THE ORGANIC HORSE

To those who set the seeds,
And those who fertilised them:
May their lips never be dry
And their horses never be touched by poisons

THE ORGANIC

PETER GRAY

HORSE

The natural management of horses explained

David & Charles

Acknowledgments

I wish to thank all of the following for their help in collecting material for this book. The generosity of both friends and strangers was something to warm the heart; as was, by and large, the response of officialdom. I apologise to anyone I may have left out.

Paul Gray for finding much of the human medical material

Ken Hill, Christchurch, who found most of the New Zealand statistics

Patricia Morris and Patrick Conlon; Anne Dean; Stuart Hutchings

Elwyn Hartley Edwards, a fount of interesting figures

Ian Mole of Equine Marketing

Judith Draper, *The British Horse*

Dr John Matthews, BVet Med, PhD, MRCVS, MAFF

Liza Moakes, MAFF Census and Surveys Office

Tim Cordes, DVM, USDA (US Department of Agriculture)

Caroline Kelly, Central Statistics Office, Dublin

Jim Linehan, Central Statistics Office, Cork

Anthony Wakeham, British Equestrian Trade Association

RCVS Wellcome Library Staff

John Digby, Keeper of the Stud Book, Randwick, NSW

John J. Cooney, The Jockey Club, Lexington, USA

Justin Blackburne, Keeper of the Stud Book, New Zealand Racing Conference

Di Spruce, Weatherbys, UK

Molly Chaffinch, American Horse Council

Denzil O'Brien, The Equestrian Federation of Australia

New Zealand Department of Statistics

Professor Reuben Rose DVSe, PhD, FRCVS, Rural Industries Research and Development Corporation, New South Wales

Photo acknowledgments

Bob Langrish: pp2–3, 7, 8, 9, 11(btm), 12, 13, 14, 17, 18, 25, 29, 31, 36(btm), 38–9, 45, 47, 54, 56, 67(btm), 75(top), 81, 87, 106, 107, 108, 116, 119, 129, 131, 134, 139, 144, 148, 150

Natural History Museum: page 10

Imperial War Museum: page 16

Kit Houghton: pp19, 23, 26, 48(right), 50, 53(right), 57, 75(btm), 86, 103, 109, 110, 112, 113, 114, 121, 127, 142, 147(btm), 151, 153, 157

Allsport: page 20

Dr D.C. Knottenbelt, University of Liverpool Department of Veterinary Clinical Science and Animal Husbandry: pp30, 34, 35, 36(top&centre), 58, 82, 123, 124, 141, 147(top)

Peter Gray: 132

Andrew Carter: pp41, 46, 53(left), 122

Still Pictures: pp42, p48(left), 64, 65, 67(top), 92, 98, 100,

Environmental Images: page 43

Garden Picture Library: page 60

The Times: page 115

Illustration on page 28 by Paul Bale/Visual Image

Illustration on page 66 from *The Chernobyl Catastrophe (Great Disasters)* by Graham Rickard (Wayland, 1988)

Illustration on page 101 from *Green Facts – the Greenhouse Effect and other Key Issues* by Michael Allaby (Hamlyn)

A DAVID & CHARLES BOOK

Hardback first published in the UK in 2001 by David & Charles
Paperback first published 2002

Distributed in North America
by F&W Publications, Inc.
4700 E. Galbraith Rd.
Cincinnati, OH 45236
1-800-289-0963
ISBN 0 7153 1401 7

Book design by Visual Image
Printed in Taiwan by Sino
for David & Charles
Brunel House   Newton Abbot   Devon

CONTENTS

Introduction

To most of us, the idea of an organic horse may conjure up dreams of wild herds of long-maned colts running the plains – and indeed, there is no intention here of drawing any different analogy. The term 'organic horse' is taken as it might for the 'organically produced cow', except, perhaps, we accept more readily here that the provision of pure water is not easy, given the extent of environmental pollution. The idea is to define what might be achieved in ideal circumstances; and to contrast, and question, what modern production and management might possibly be asking the animal to endure. In a way, the exercise is an examination of conscience, and an inquiry into exactly what we are doing to the horse today.

The term 'organic' in animal production means the provision of a system of rearing and growing that is free from the use of artificial fertilisers, sprays for plant diseases, and that protects animals from man-made toxic contaminants – such as those emitted from factories and brought down by rain into water supplies. It requires a particular set of farming principles laid out in this book and standards of produce purity the same as those asked of organic farmers by The Soil Association.

As we enter the new millennium, a modern swell of interest has spawned an industry of horse-related trades and services that shows no sign of abating. The horse, as part of our daily lives, is as infectious to us as are some of the diseases that enter the equation and detract at least a little from the pleasure. The material side of this means a constant stream of innovations, some of which are of benefit to the animal, and some that are not. There are always new products and new fashions.

We have come from a time when the idea of organic feeding was as prevalent and natural as the lack of it seems today. This ended, probably, in the late sixties and early seventies, when there was a renewed upsurge in horse numbers. The nucleus of this, as far as European breeding was concerned, started in County Cork, Ireland, where the fledgling Coolmore and Rathbarry Stud operations were already forming. In the US the process was already under way, and in short order, Australia, and then New Zealand, followed.

The first Irish breeders I met would proudly show off pastures that had never in living memory been ploughed or had artificial products spread on them. The field of oats (only for their horses) was grown without fertiliser or pesticide, prayers were said that it would be saved without rain, and the idea that the body of an athletic animal should be polluted by any unidentified drug or chemical was unacceptable. The growth of vital bone and muscle had to be nurtured in a manner as close to that designed by nature as was physically possible. It was a quality of thought we seem to have dispensed with today.

Nowadays many owners don't have the luxury of vast acres, or the opportunity to grow their own cereals, and most are lucky to have even small paddocks in which to allow their animals a daily browse. Both feed and bedding have to be bought in, and there is little owner control over quality or content. The production of bulk materials that must make a profit for the producer usually means that crops are grown by the standards of modern intensive farming; thus grasses are helped by dressings of nitrogen and other chemicals, and the grain may well have been sprayed with pesticide and herbicide, or been genetically altered. Increasingly Man's intrusion on nature is all-encompassing.

The purpose of this book is to draw attention to the natural horse, and to show how the presence of substances it eats may affect its body systems, lower its immunity, influence the spread of disease and affect performance. People involved with racehorses and those in active competition will, in particular, be aware of the problems imposed by infection. It is growing in prevalence, and is a factor which increasingly is limiting the use of the horse, especially for competitive purposes. Its insidious spread is evident, and it becomes a problem for even the leisure horse owner when conditions like 'flu or strangles are about. Affected horses may stand sick in their paddocks or stalls, and in the most extreme circumstances may even die or have to be destroyed. The causal organisms may be spat into the wind, they may be contacted from horses passing on the roads, or from the hands and clothes of the people who tend them.

Colic is a case in point, and can affect any horse, either at grass or in the stable. It is a condition that costs lives, often after unendurable pain and suffering, and it is frequently

The ponies of the New Forest introduce variety to their diet by nibbling on gorse bushes and other leafy vegetation

diet-related; moreover science suggests there is an increasing incidence of gastric and intestinal ulcers in horses. What this means is that such problems are preventable. We need to simplify our approach to feeding and get away from the commerical influences that are, in all probability, exacerbating the problem. If we can revert to the organic standards of our ancestors, there is no doubt we can reduce disease and have more healthy horses that can perform to their ability over a longer timespan.

Our purpose is to draw attention to these problems. While there are Codes of Practice and International Regulations for disease control, these can be above the heads of many horse owners. That is why it is important that we should identify the causes, explain the reasoning and show the way to control and prevention. Organic standards naturally have these aims.

At the end of the exercise, the creation of awareness is what it's all about. In practical terms it may be difficult for the average person to control the quality of intakes, and as a result organic standards may be an ideal not easily reached. However, to know is to be wise, and any move in the right direction can only be of universal benefit to the horse.

To date, the principles of intensive horse production have usually allowed expansion without any thought of the pitfalls –

The Connemara pony is remarkably hardy, and originates from the wild, empty part of Ireland lying to the west of Loughs Mask and Corrib

indeed, the thinking seems to be that unseen problems can always be relieved when they come, through the application of science. This, however, is too far from the ideal, and it is better to anticipate diseases and to avoid them. This is possible if we put limits on intensive systems before they start. In the domesticated kingdom there is always the opportunity to plan and control, although this is a lesson we seem particularly slow to recognise. However, failure to do so not only leads to disease, but to standards of animal welfare that are sometimes unacceptable.

NOTE

Throughout the course of the book it may be considered that there is too much comparison between human and horse diseases: there are those who say that no comparison is ever justified, and that man is man and the horse is an animal, with no similarities. But this argument does not fit, because many diseases are very similar, both in the way they arise and the symptoms that are produced. There are direct comparisons between the way different body systems work. For instance the lungs of a human athlete and those of an animal athlete have very similar demands placed on them, and there are huge anatomical similarities, even if the horse stands on four legs against our two. The functioning of the muscular and skeletal systems is comparable too, even allowing for the different ways in which stresses lead to injury and lameness. The way in which horses succumb to and suffer from infectious diseases is similar; and finally the protective mechanisms are based on the same principles. That is not to say there are no differences – but neither is it to say the glass is so fogged that we cannot see the essentials.

1 Wild Versus Field Conditions

All who love horses will have a concept of the animal of bygone times roaming vast plains: quick-moving, dangerous, beautiful, in many ways like the wild mustangs of the American plains often seen on film, though different. Running in small groups, they might have consisted of a dominant stallion and his band of mares, with perhaps foals and other youngstock in tow. Watching constantly for predators, they ran from dangers and fought those that poached their grazing areas.

The true original horse, as palaeontologists inform us, was *Eohippus*. This small, dog-like creature dated back millions of years and was very different from the horse we now know. In fact for a long time North America – as indeed much of the western hemisphere – was free of horses. There are several theories as to why this might have been, but the fact is that horses only reappeared in North America after the visits of the Spaniards in the sixteenth century. The first record is of Hernan Cortés who landed in Mexico in 1519 with sixteen horses, beginning the repopulation. The mustang is therefore a modern phenomenon, actually a feral horse that escaped from domestication and established itself in the wild in later years.

The earliest fossilised remains of *Eohippus* date back fifty-four million years and were found in Wyoming and Utah; it was only evident some four million years later in Europe. It was a mere 25–50cm (10–20in) high, and was a browsing forest dweller, eating leaves and soft shoots of undergrowth – types of food likely to provide quick energy through digestion in the small bowel. It had a smaller head than the horse we know, an arched back, an elongated snout and a fine tail. With four digits on each foreleg and three on each hind leg, large tough pads bore its weight and kept the toes off the ground. Its teeth were more like those of a dog, and it took many millions of years of evolution to transform this creature into the animal of today.

▼ *The diminutive* Eohippus, *once known as* Hyracotherium

The advent of grasses on the great plains led to changes in both its lifestyle and its anatomy, eventually resulting in the tooth design and body structure we are familiar with. The scourge of predatory wolf packs led to the changes in lower limb anatomy that produced the single-digited horse, *Equus caballus*, largely because speed had become critical for escape. Gradually there was an increase in body size; a bigger head housed a bigger brain, and widening of the facial sinuses placed the eyes to the side, giving a broader field of vision. Also the ears evolved so they moved in an

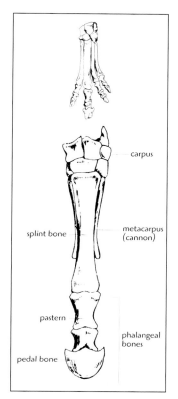

Compare the four digits of Eohippus *(top) with the single digit of today's horse*

Labels on diagram: carpus, splint bone, metacarpus (cannon), pastern, phalangeal bones, pedal bone

arc and were thus able to detect sound from behind as well as in front.

Today's digit (comprising the cannon, fetlock, pastern and foot) is equivalent to the third digit of *Eohippus*, or the central digit of the human hand. The lost second and fourth digits are represented by the small splint bones at either side of the central cannon; the remains of the first digit is still seen in the form of the chestnut. These changes brought greater speed off the mark, but at the cost of some structural weaknesses, as we shall see later.

The horse is unique in that within the process of evolution it was provided with a means of staying upright while sleeping: this is the stay apparatus, a system of tendons and ligaments capable of locking the limbs while resting and so eliminating the need to lie down. The benefit lay in that the horse was thus in a better state of preparedness to take flight; and the development of a more athletic frame made escape from predators more possible.

In summary, the constant change was towards greater size, more speed and increased strength as the horse adapted from being a forest browser to an herbivorous range dweller. A voluminous large bowel was the key to digesting fibre and providing an energy source to replace the leaves and the shoots. But the ranges were more exposed than the forests, and there was a need to be ever vigilant and to cover long distances to find grazing and water.

CONDITIONS IN THE WILD

Did the original horse have a healthy and disease-free existence? After all, there was no pollution as we know it, coming from factories and vehicle emissions. There were, of course, the more serious results of volcanoes and earthquakes to be contended with as well as the hazard of comets, and these, it is suspected, may have wiped out whole species of animals at times. A particular disaster was the eruption of Mount Toba in Sumatra some 70,000 years ago. Huge volumes of ash were sent up, causing a volcanic winter that blotted out the sun, a climatic state that lasted six years and lowered temperatures radically, killing as much as 75 per cent of plants. It was followed by a thousand-year ice age that wiped out many other forms of life, the main areas of survival being in Africa, Europe and Asia. Another complicating factor would have been radically changing sea levels, probably resulting from any of the above disasters.

Australian Brumbies are generally degenerated ('scrub') horses descended from domestic species gone wild

But, such happenings excepted, can we suggest that there was only a benign nature to be contended with? That life was an easy and sedentary option, except for the risk of predators? The answer, of course, is no, and there were many other hazards, as there always will be. It has even been suggested that the loss of horses from the West might have been due to plague or pestilence. This is unlikely, although the oldest recognised sign of life is a fossilised bacterial cell said to be about three billion years old, therefore suggesting that the means existed. But survivors would always be expected after problems of that kind, from which new populations would emerge.

There is so much that we don't know. Moving to more modern times, it is known that a flu-like infection created serious problems long before viruses were capable of being identified; so diseases existed and animals suffered them.

Nature's Design In designing any animal, Nature, we might imagine, was the greatest of all idealists. Forever learning from changing circumstances, bodies were engineered with the most specific structures and designs needed to adapt to the habitat in hand. Anatomical systems had to be fed with the precise means of their growth and fuelling, and from available sources. But Nature was also, always, a pragmatist. She was cruel to the weak and injured, who were sacrificed to feed those placed lower on the pecking order – there was never a question of mercy. In her drive for perfection, she has always balanced the scales without pity. Indeed, if she did not, the world we know might never have lasted as long as it has; thus she could never have allowed weak animals, and that included horses, to transmit genes that might have weakened the species.

▼ *These mustangs have to forage for their food on the plains of Nevada, USA*

Food The horse on the plains had to forage for his food against all the odds, and that included the ravages of tempests, the threat of drought and the constant danger of shortage. Failure to find enough to eat, and of an adequate nutritional quality, could only lead to poor body growth for the young and infection for the old. The need for

△ *Wild horses, such as these mustangs in Colorado, USA, tend to leave their droppings in piles to avoid contaminating grazing areas*

water was constant and demanding, and like now, water holes could run dry. It was inevitably a precarious existence, and one from which there was no escape.

Then, as now, there was a need for strong bone that would keep an animal mobile and sound, but this depended on eating herbage containing enough calcium and phosphorus, the principal minerals of bone: if either was in short supply, as well as other basic items, existence itself was put at risk. There also had to be enough protein to build muscle, and enough carbohydrate to generate the energy for routine activities, including flight and everyday travel. Even as today, the quality of growing herbage could vary from season to season, and if there were large numbers of other consumers, the table could easily have been eaten bare.

Disease   Wild horses might have been saved the pest of parasitic worms, though that would have depended on how many were grazing any one area, and how long they stayed in it; and it would also have depended on a means of transmission, as horses are naturally clean in their habits and do not graze soiled land if at all possible. On the American ranges, the mustangs leave their droppings in piles, and it has to be assumed that this type of behaviour is based in nature and might even trace back to the earliest beginnings. But parasites prolong their existence through overcoming such obstacles, and there are ways in which this can be done. An intermediate host would be one answer, as the liver fluke of today (which uses a snail); or the botfly that lays its eggs on the horse's hair, from where they are licked, thus gaining access to the body. Of course, some horses are known to eat faeces, but it has to be imagined that this is an aberration; in domestication it is mostly foals that behave in this way, and it is thought that they need to do this in order to produce a healthy flora of digestive organisms.

The Camargue ponies in the south of France live in a practically wild state on the marshy lands around the mouth of the Rhône

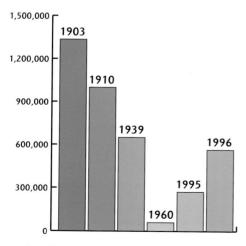

Horses on agricultural holdings in the twentieth century – Great Britain (NB 1996 figures indicate total horse population)

Horses might also have avoided a great deal of the bacterial and viral diseases we worry about today. This would have depended on many things, such as periods of drought, or floods, or population numbers. The reality is that infection has always been a result of any factor – even hunger or age – that might threaten the immune state of man or beast. More than now, though, malnourished foals never got a chance to develop in the wild, whereas we are in a position to pamper them. Similarly, animals too old to run were at the quick mercy of the predators.

THE MODERN HORSE

The major difference today is that the horse we know is a product of domestication. What does that mean? At one level it means a taming of wild instincts, a familiarity with the human race; at another it means control. Basically, in order to get what we want, we provide food, shelter and training, inviting this usually willing and nicely tempered animal into our lives. The purpose may be transport or draught work, and in some cases the horse is still a source of human food. But the essence of what exists is a relationship best expressed from the saddle – though even from on the ground, it can be closer than that which we enjoy with any other fierce and powerful beast. And there is no doubting the horse can be fearsome: we dare not pit our meagre strength against it, only our guile; as anyone who has ever got into a battle with one will know, there can only be one winner. But there is also, on the other hand, a great deal of love to be had from this animal.

Equus caballus is thought to have made its first appearance in Central Asia. The earliest recorded use of horses as a means of transport was from the Sumerians of Southern Mesopotamia, 4,000 to 5,000 years ago. They moved goods by means of vehicles drawn by onagers, or wild asses, but *Equus* did not appear in North America until Hernan Cortés. And yet by about 1914 it was estimated that there were about 25,000,000 horses in total in North America. Midway through the previous century, the number of wild horses was estimated to be between 3,000,000 and 5,000,000, but this had dropped to something in the region of 1,000,000 by the turn of the new century, because of fencing on the great plains. The mule population went from 559,000 in 1850 to a staggering 5,432,000 in 1920 – the most in the world.

Now, the figure for wild horses is maintained at about 45,000. Today there are 800,000 Quarter Horses in the US, and

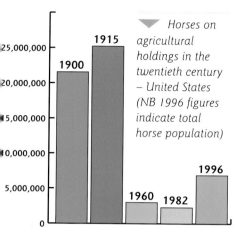

Horses on agricultural holdings in the twentieth century – United States (NB 1996 figures indicate total horse population)

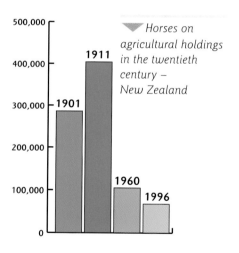

Horses on agricultural holdings in the twentieth century – New Zealand

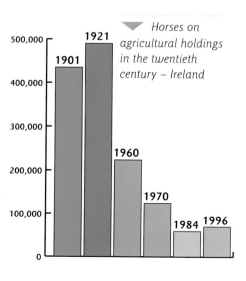

Horses on agricultural holdings in the twentieth century – Ireland

it is the most numerous breed; in fact a survey in 1996, conducted by the American Horse Council, placed the current figure at 6.9 million horses in all. And in Britain today, according to the BETA National Equestrian survey of 1996, there are 575,000 horses in all, of which 65,000 are classed as being within the professional sector (this latter figure includes Thoroughbreds, and competition horses and ponies). Compare this to the turn of the century, when 300,000 horses worked in London alone. There were 1,000,000 farm horses in England and Wales at their peak in 1910, though this figure had dropped to about 60,000 by 1960. But they were different times, and the priorities of the day meant so many things back then.

The Horse in the Near Past It is worth recalling the role of the horse in the society of a century ago. Firstly, it held a critical position in everyday life, helping to farm the land as well as transporting goods and bodies in cities and the countryside. There was also leisure riding – for instance, hunting was popular – though equestrian sport was in its infancy and largely held back by the limitations of transport. More importantly, the horse was a vital element in the working of armies, in the operation of war. Consider 1,000,000 Allied cavalry horses positioned behind the fronts in 1916, and in 1939 the Russian Army had 1,200,000 horses. Huge numbers were lost in battle – for example, 500,000 British horses were lost on the Western Front in the Great War.

Records tell us that in those times, husbandry was of varied standards. As films of the American West remind us, the riding horse was loved and cared for, and as hard in fitness as any of today's training methods will enable a horse to be; and as man's

Australia	No figures available	1 TB mare per 600 people
Irish Republic	1 horse per 50 people	1 TB mare per 350 people
New Zealand	1 horse per 53 people	1 TB mare per 450 people
UK	1 horse per 100 people	1 TB mare per 6,000 people
USA	1 horse per 40 people	1 TB mare per 7,500 people
Note:	There was 1 horse per 3 people in the USA in 1914	
	There was 1 horse per 3 people in New Zealand in 1911	
	There was 1 horse per 7 people in Ireland in 1901	
	No total horse population available for the UK at that time	

Horses per head of population today

The role of the horse has changed enormously since the early twentieth century: huge numbers were lost during World War I

closest companion, it was thoughtfully fed and watered, shod and bedded. On the other hand, there is a suggestion that working horses kept in large city depots were sometimes packed into steamy conditions that were neither clean nor hygienic – bacterial infections were rife, and there were no antibiotics to treat them with. Many of the conditions were fatal – as they were with humans. Luckily we don't see them nowadays, besides which we have the benefit of a wide range of treatments, and fewer instances of the steamy conditions.

Domestication and its Effects Contrast the horse in the wild with the situation it faces today: there are important differences. Still designed by the idealist in Nature, our horse is confined to grazing land of strictly finite borders. Furthermore, stable yards are getting bigger and changing in character, and man decides the diet, dictates exercise routines and controls disease. There is a whole commercial industry growing around the animal, dealing in everything from goods to education.

The effects of management changes are seen in the way diseases are moving. Forever pushing for better performance and the breaking of records, breeders want a stronger and quicker animal. As bigger horses are seen to be more vulnerable to injury, size is not a factor, but we look for more precocious growth and speed beyond the natural capacity of Nature to provide it. The result is, veterinary science suggests, more disease of growing bone; those involved in clinical practice also see infection increase from year to year.

Modern Management There is a growing tendency to be over-innovative in relation to feeding, something which will be considered in coming chapters. Some of this is propelled by commercial interests. Furthermore, the influences on food quality of intensive production and environmental pollution are significant and worrying, specifically because they challenge the horse's natural digestive system.

The movement in stabling is towards larger buildings, with critical changes in design and environment control. The need of these is dictated by economic factors, as well as convenience and the comfort of workers. There is also a wide range of cheap wooden structures that are often cold, draughty and uninsulated, and a secondary consideration must be that horses might suffer in such conditions. Thus our attempts at comparing the needs of the stabled horse with the animal in the wild, and providing for him adequately, lacks insight; we shall try later to throw some light on the way this is.

The number of horses per acre is on the rise, too, as much as the size of private paddocks is getting smaller. This is partly because of urbanisation – the 'horse in the garden' syndrome – but it also has to do with economics, again. Land is forever more costly, especially in and around cities; but even in the countryside, an acre now costs multiples of what it did after the last war. Signs of more intensive horse management are to be seen on stud farms, and in racing establishments and competition yards. Another worrying factor is that instead of old pastures, unploughed in living memory, we see increasingly the combined influences of forced grasses and increased stocking rates. Essentially this means a greater use of artificial fertilisers, which has recognised disadvantages. These and pesticides have long been thought essential to, respectively, increase production and control plant disease – but research has repeatedly pointed out to us that toxicity is limited.

If these substances are toxic to marine mammals, which is proven, who can say that

A modern stable complex and walker, typical of many racing establishments and competition yards today

they do not have a tissue-damaging effect on animals closer to the source? They may not cause overt clinical disease in horses, but do they accumulate in the liver like they do in seals, for example? To what effect? Do they influence immunity, especially in the maximally trained animal? Can they affect mineral balances? What of unwanted oestrogenic substances, like those thought to be affecting the sexuality of bears at the North Pole?

Yet another factor worth bearing in mind is that in intensive conditions, the interval between worming treatments becomes, in real terms, ever shorter; thus people who formerly dosed just once or twice a year now do it every six to eight weeks. Furthermore with growing numbers, infectious and epidemic diseases tend to become more prevalent. Even with good nutrition, large numbers of horses kept in close contact offer opportunities to disease-causing organisms that they don't have otherwise. The greatest danger lies not only in new diseases, of which there have been several in modern times, but also in the emergence of new expressions of those we already know. The effects of all this have to be assessed with the specific needs of the athletic animal in mind.

The reality is that today's civilisation tends to learn by its mistakes. We expand first, and face the consequences afterwards, especially when dealing with an animal that is not, for the most of us, a food producer. Because of this, the horse does not have the importance as a subject of research that the cow has, for example: basically it does not warrant the funding. Consequently our knowledge is often poor, despite new sources of finance, and this is a situation towards which current commercial concerns are unlikely to change their attitude.

Keeping too many horses in a limited space can lead to many health and management problems

Thoroughbred horses are now a currency in which much wealth is vested

The Thoroughbred Since its emergence, the Thoroughbred has been pre-eminent among modern athletic horses. Its forerunners were the Byerley Turk, born in 1679; the Darley Arabian, born in 1700; and the Godolphin Barb, born in 1724; and ever since then it has fuelled Man's fantasies and gained his admiration for its strength, its athleticism and its sheer beauty. In fact it is probably the Thoroughbred and its attractive qualities that has re-awakened interest in the horse in the modern world; and it is certainly through the Thoroughbred that the increase in the horse population since the sixties has come about. The growth in other breeds, marked by the increasing pursuit of leisure riding, has simply followed a path that moves forward on an almost annual basis. It reflects Man's deep love and admiration for the horse, a love that knows few boundaries, as horses are deep in our blood – and even those who claim otherwise are not really being true, since their objections are usually not to the animal. The constant increase of interest stands as proof of this, and it is often the children of those who object that express the change.

The future is impeded only by economic influences, and as always, money dictates value as well as maintenance costs. Thus at the upper end of the Thoroughbred market, horses are now a currency for the rich to deal in. An owner one day described an over-valued mare as a 'gusher' – an oil well that generated money; yet oil is more likely to hold its value than an animal which, in the end, may only be worth its weight as flesh. Sadly, there are still many who are prepared to beggar themselves for the follies of this seductive affair, and too many young people aspire to make a living out of what essentially should be a hobby. We can expect the horse to thrive only as long as society has the means to afford it.

The Wider Scene There are distinct parallels between human and equine disease conditions, largely because there are important biological similarities. Also, we consume the same water, and many of our foods come from the same land. The horse, of course, is a herbivore, and we would hope consumes no product of animal origin. But the sprays and dressings that are used in farming are as likely to affect horses as they are North Pole bears and people, and it is widely accepted that they can damage the health.

The horse as an athlete suffers many of the stresses and physical breakdowns that human athletes suffer. Medical science recognises a link between infection and intensive training – thus human athletes are often subject to training disruption over long periods because of low-grade infection, and the same happens to horses.

The horse also suffers from similar physical conditions to human athletes, and the extension of chiropractic manipulation and physiotherapy into the treatment of horses is a clear statement of this. While there are evident anatomical differences, the similarities are many and it is important to recognise them. The horse will, ultimately, benefit.

Physical injuries suffered by human athletes have strict parallels in horses

Equine Medicine From the days when veterinary medicine emerged out of the wider influences of farriery, today's profession is an evolved, and evolving, science. More diseases are recognised, and more are effectively treated, but we have not progressed to a point where we are able to prevent or eradicate the common conditions fully. There is a need for much more quality clinical feedback, and for much more practical work in areas such as feeding and stabling, where we tend to follow a lot of loose principles without ever getting to grips with the basics.

Diseases of bone and cartilage have resulted from the production of more precocious and heavier stock, and science sees these conditions on the increase. Some were not recognised more than a generation ago, but now we need to be able to link cause and effect.

WHAT YOU CAN DO

HOW WE CAN INFLUENCE OUR HORSE'S WELFARE

1 **On the whole** we can fully control our horses' digestive inputs as well as their living conditions.

2 **We have the choice** as to whether or not we want an organic standard for them.

3 **Organic food** will only become available if there is a significant demand, and producers who wish to meet the demand.

4 **The justification** for an organic system of management is in how we wish our horses to grow and develop; our aiming to keep them free from preventable disease; and in the quality of performance we seek.

5 **We can,** in fact, control virtually everything that happens to our horses in their lives, including housing standards, exercise and freedom to roam.

6 **We can dictate** the quality of what our horses drink, though an individual owner has no control over what comes down in the rain or what might be added to, or seep into, water supplies.

7 **In pursuing** the organic ideal, it can never be our aim to push Nature to the limit by increasing stocking rates and waiting to see if there is an increase in disease; this is the way progress mostly comes under intensive systems.

8 **We must realise** that cruelty is the inflicting of disease by means that could, or should, be avoided.

9 **No predictable level** of animal disease is acceptable under the organic philosophy.

10 **Disease is avoided** by planning, by consideration, and by placing limits on intensive production.

2 | Natural Digestion

While the horse's digestive system is well understood, aspects of how it works are especially important in considering the organic concept. As with most things, knowing the normal helps us recognise the abnormal, especially when environmental or production factors might change the nature of food, which in turn might affect Nature's design for a healthy animal. The question is: are we feeding (or creating in the environment) materials that might make it impossible for the digestive system to function normally?

THE NATURAL PROCESS

Digestion is a complex matter, converting even the simplest of diets (like hay and oats) into protein, carbohydrate and fat. Minerals, vitamins and trace elements are extracted and absorbed into the bloodstream; amino acids are produced as well as vitamins, such as vitamin B12, that are not available from dietary sources.

The digestive process is assisted by the action of specific enzymes, of which there are as many as 10,000 types in the body. These are the chemical catalysts of most reactions, vital to digestion, and active in every individual cell of the body. Life would not exist without them because body structures could not be built or maintained, nor could energy be produced. For digestive enzymes to work, there is a correct acid or alkaline medium needed, and this varies from one segment of the gut to another; anything disturbing the balance is capable of creating a digestive upset.

pH Values pH is a measure of the degree to which a solution is acid or alkaline. At a pH of 7.0 a solution is neutral – that is, neither acid nor alkaline; as the figure drops below 7.0 it becomes more acid in nature, and the reverse also applies. Water is generally close to neutral, although rainwater has a pH in the range of 5.5–6.5. Some acid rain has been recorded with a pH as low as 2.6 (about as low as it gets in the stomach). The pH of blood is in the range of 7.3–7.5.

pH within the gut is affected by the production of substances such as saliva and the fluid from the pancreas, which are alkaline; and acids, such as hydrochloric acid which is found in the stomach, as well as fatty acids produced in quantity in the large intestine. The type of enzyme released in each bowel area, and the effect it will have on breaking down food substances, is, as we have already said, dependent on pH. The food a horse eats – even the simplest grasses – needs to be broken down like this before it can be of use in maintaining body structure, and able to provide energy for movement as well as other vital functions.

Sheep help to clean pastures horses graze on, and play a valuable part in parasite control

THE STOMACH

The horse, unlike the cow and sheep, has a single stomach. A relatively small, single organ, it accounts for something in the region of 10 per cent of abdominal space – and this is unlikely to have changed much from the days of *Eohippus*. In contrast, cattle have four large stomach compartments taking up most of the abdomen. The reason for a smaller size is explained by the nature of the horse, by the need for mobility and speed, as a large, heavy stomach would inevitably be a handicap when needing to move at short notice, maybe over long distances. The overall design allows for the provision of quick energy from materials such as succulent grasses which have been digested and absorbed in the stomach and small bowel. Creating energy from fibre is a slower process, being brought about further down the bowel.

How Herbivores Differ One interesting difference between cattle and horses is that cattle store large quantities of herbage in their first stomach, and regurgitate it for chewing and mixing with saliva. This 'chewing the cud' happens while the animal is recumbent and at rest. The horse, which sleeps while standing and does not have the same need to lie down, grazes almost continually and there is no regurgitation. This is its nature, and the difference in the two types of digestion from the same food sources is quite remarkable.

Acid Medium and Ulcers The medium in the stomach is largely acid, which is essential for the action of the enzymes there. In the end nearest the gullet, the influence of saliva lowers acidity (pH rises), but it rises as the small intestine is reached (pH falls). The protein-digesting enzyme known as pepsin is important in the stomach, although the absorption of protein occurs mainly in the small bowel; however, pepsin has its effect in an acid medium. Also, the macerating influence of the acid plays an important role in the breakdown of food components.

The lining of the stomach is protected from its own acid, and from digestion by its enzymes – at least in part – by a thick coating of mucus. The development of ulcers is seen as a failure of this protection, though the problem would appear to be considerably more involved than that. Ulcers are now thought to be on the increase, and the causes have to be aligned to changed feeding practices and to our failure to understand the correct management of the digestive system.

The Intestines

The small intestine, to where the partly digested food passes after the stomach, is buffered by large volumes of alkaline fluid from the pancreas. This comes with a quantity of enzymes, the efficient action of which will depend on a reduction of acidity (or a higher pH). Trypsin, a protein-digesting enzyme there, has its effect in an alkaline medium. The same applies to enzymes for carbohydrate and fat digestion.

A Bulky Bowel The size of the large bowel varies with diet. Horses on a high quantity of fibre, fed plenty of coarse hay, and perhaps eating their bedding, tend to have a voluminous bowel – and this is a disadvantage in strong (or fast) work, since the very bulk and weight is a handicap, quite apart from the fact that it creates forward pressure on the diaphragm; this interferes with expansion of the lungs and can cause breathing difficulties. The effect, like a fat-bellied man in a race, is to reduce exercise tolerance, limit performance, and make the affected animal blow hard when it pulls up after work. This can all be prevented by controlling fibre intake and providing concentrate feeds – though care must be taken not to starve the gut organisms and thereby cause greater problems. The addition of oils, a recent innovation, may further increase energy content without significantly increasing total feed bulk. But is there a cost to the animal?

Hay Quality Poor-quality hay causes excessive fermentation – partly, at least, because of bringing with it a large quantity of yeasts and fungi – and leads to performance problems by increasing large bowel size. It also causes gas production in other areas. This is quickly resolved when recognised, however, and the bad hay replaced with some of better quality. Horses that eat their bedding are similarly affected.

The Importance of Fibre In the large bowel, bacterial fermentation and other processes allow for digestion of a diet that must have a high percentage of fibre. The physical presence of fibre is essential to stimulate bowel activity throughout: it provokes peristalsis, a type of running muscle contraction that pushes the food contents forward – without this, food would accumulate and impact, and digestion would not proceed. Equally important, fibre is a specific food for the bacterial and protozoal organisms that inhabit the large bowel and are central to digestion. Without them, fibre would not be broken down, and its essential nutritive value would not be made available for use.

BACTERIAL DIGESTION

As just mentioned, fibrous food is broken down by organisms in order to complete the process of digestion. This is essential, and occurs in both the stomach and small intestine, though it is more important as a feature of large bowel digestion.

Indigestible Fibre Problems arise where the diet is made up of indigestible fibres. The horse does not possess an enzyme system, for example, that might allow it to digest lignin, contained in wood, straw and hulls. Lignin is formed in herbage as it ages: it may be chewed and macerated, but it will not be digested, and then the organisms of the bowel will not survive. Their demand is constant and on-going, and any continued deficiency of fibre will lead to their loss, even over a matter of hours.

The Death of Gut Organisms When the normal digestive organisms die, they are likely to be replaced by disease-causing bacteria; this can even lead to death in conditions such as colitis X, which sometimes occurs when horses are moved from poor to rich pastures. New food entering the digestive system is thought to be the triggering factor. It could be that inadequate fibre is the cause, or the infection could be due to exposure to the growth of a foreign organism, such as Salmonella. It's a 'catch 22' situation, in that either the loss of normal organisms, and the consequences of this, are the irritant; or disease is caused by outside organisms overcoming and replacing them.

If any of the processes in the stomach and small intestine are not operating properly, diarrhoea could result, because the food is not adequately broken down for subsequent normal digestion; this could lead to death from the effects of acute fluid loss. Alternatively, a digestive disturbance might lead to anorexia (no will to eat). The body would then be left to evacuate existing waste and recover through a gradual resumption of normal feeding. However, death could result from infection, especially if toxins were produced by a foreign organism; or as a result of complete stagnation. Alternatively, there could be severe, but treatable, constipation.

Insufficient Fibre A risk exists, where grasses are young and contain insufficient fibre, that the large bowel will be without

This forward grass (ie in a state of advanced growth) has plenty of fibre

CASE NOTE

To explain digestive disturbance further, it might be helpful to draw from a real experience. Some years ago, a small team of stallions showed a tendency to diarrhoea every time a new batch of feed was introduced. The stud owner asked for a letter to send to the manufacturers in support of a complaint. Being less wise than now, I addressed the letter 'To whom it may concern'. The essence of the message was that different batches of feed varied in content. Some even differed in colour, supporting the suggestion that they contained different constituents. The outcome, for the stallions, was digestive upset, which was worrying during the peak of their working season, with no rest possible for them.

There was a worry, too, about dehydration, as well as the clear fear that the problem could cause debilitating illness.

The feed company were so disturbed they took immediate legal advice. Fearing the possible publication of the letter, they readily accepted it might do serious damage to their business. Counsel's advice was, as I had no scientific proof to support the allegations, I would be liable for any damages suffered. However, it was a very valuable group of stallions. The claim, if any had been lost, might well have equalled their loss if the letter had been published.

The lesson is the folly of not knowing what is being fed to horses.

adequate mechanical stimulus. Then, too, the native organisms may be starved, bringing a significant reduction in numbers; and, as we said, they might be replaced with disease-causing organisms. Laminitis, it is suspected, may be precipitated this way.

Enzyme Failure The failure of an enzyme in the stomach or small intestine might lead to inadequately broken-down material entering the large bowel. This food will arrive in an undecomposed and indigestible condition; the organisms will be unable to handle it and have nothing to feed off. Something similar happens when there is carbohydrate overload (the horse that raids the feed bin, or is overfed on concentrates). The outcome could be infection, toxin production, or other expressions of digestive disturbance such as diarrhoea, constipation, even colic.

Samples of pelleted feed may vary between batches, even from the same supplier

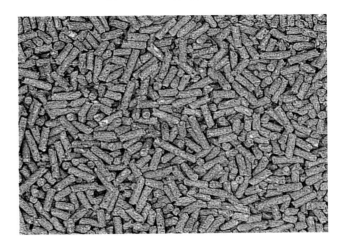

Feed Consistency It is important that feed is consistent for optimum digestibility. Compounded (or pelleted) feeds may or may not contain the same contents, from the same sources, from one batch to the next, and unless the user has full control over the constituents – in other words, unless you make your own nuts from your own raw materials – it is never possible to avoid the risk of change. In reality, you depend on the word and integrity of the producer. A supplier or compounder may only specify the protein, carbohydrate and fat percentages, and a list of minerals and vitamins in the feed, and all sorts of different combinations may produce similar figures. Different batches may contain materials from different sources. Reputable compounders, however, stake their reputation on the quality and consistency of their feeds. They are in a position to store raw materials, and they depend on the satisfaction of their clients as a means to develop their business. The possibility of trouble lies with the unscrupulous, or as a consequence of human error, or where the raw materials themselves may deteriorate or prove deficient.

For the health of the horse it is vital that there is consistency in what is fed. Disease, if only digestive upset, results from changes in diet.

VARIETY OF RAW MATERIALS CONTAINED IN TYPICAL MODERN FEEDS

Foal Creep Feed (based on oats, barley, soya bean meal, dried milk or whey, added mineral and vitamins – type and levels in the hands of the compounder)

PROTEIN 18% OIL 5% FIBRE 6% ENERGY 13.5 MJ/KG FEED

Rearing Feed for Young Growing Horses (based on oats, barley, soya, maize, peas, grass meal, alfalfa, added mineral and vitamins)

PROTEIN 15–18% OIL 3–5% FIBRE 8–14% ENERGY 12.5 MJ/KG FEED

Stud Feed for Mares in Foal and During Lactation (based on oats, barley, maize, peas, soya meal, added mineral and vitamins)

PROTEIN 12–16% OIL 3–5% FIBRE 8% ENERGY 12–13 MJ/KG FEED

Horses in Training for Racing or Competition (based on oats, barley, maize, peas, soya beans, grass meal, alfalfa, added mineral and vitamins)

PROTEIN 12–15% OIL 4–8% FIBRE 8–14% ENERGY 13.5–15 MJ/KG FEED

Hunters (based on oats, barley, maize, peas, added mineral and vitamins)

PROTEIN 10–12% OIL 3–5% FIBRE 8–19% ENERGY 12.5 MJ/KG FEED

Riding Horses not in Competition (based on oats, barley, maize, peas, linseed meal, grass meal, alfalfa, added mineral and vitamins)

PROTEIN 8–9% OIL 1–3% FIBRE 15–40% ENERGY 7–10 MJ/KG FEED

notes

Other substances – such as sugar beet, brewer's grains or yeast, various grasses, fishmeal, flax meal, peanut meal, bran, flour by-products – may be included.

Materials may be micronised (a process that includes heating and rolling in order to produce a dry and free-flowing product), cooked, chopped or pelleted, and may come as nuts or as whole-feed mixes.

Particular ingredients may be included or excluded from given formulae: for example, oats may be excluded from some mixes for horses that react to them.

All sorts of additives may be included for flavouring or other purposes, like molasses, herbs, garlic, comfrey; even yeast cultures used to promote digestive efficiency, though their usefulness is questioned on the grounds they may upset normal bacterial balance.

HOW THE HORSE EATS

A set of sharp incisor teeth tear at herbage which is guided into the mouth by the very mobile lips. The wide surfaces of the molar teeth crush ingested food while mixing it with saliva, the release of which is stimulated by the chewing. Saliva acts as a lubricant to ensure the food traverses the long oesophagus, or gullet, without causing choke. It is alkaline in nature and this, as we have seen, affects the fluid medium in the stomach. As is well recognised in man, too much acid can lead to reflux and acid indigestion, an awful burning sensation that is very uncomfortable. The same problem can occur in the horse and the alkaline saliva is an integral part of the normal control mechanism.

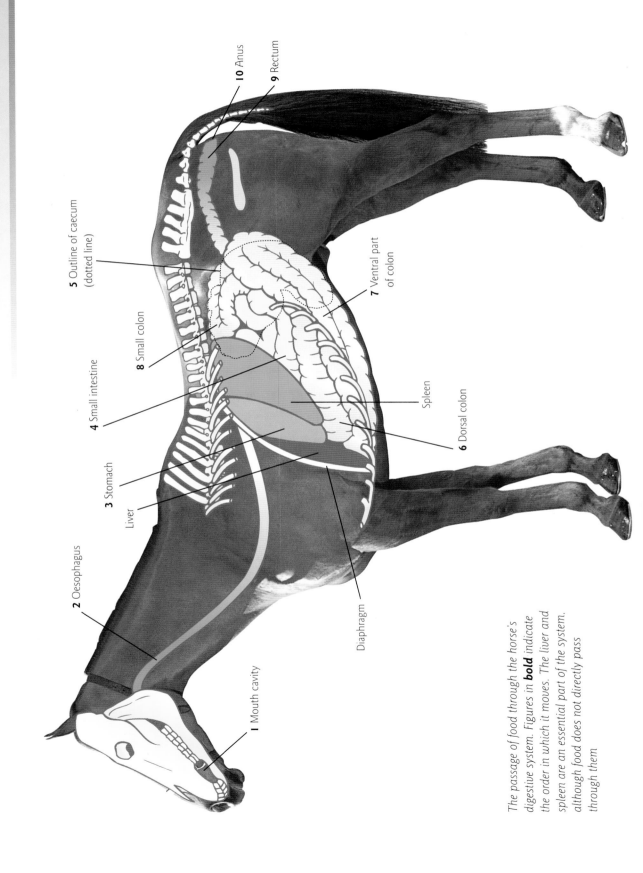

10 Anus

9 Rectum

5 Outline of caecum (dotted line)

8 Small colon

4 Small intestine

7 Ventral part of colon

3 Stomach

Liver

Spleen

6 Dorsal colon

2 Oesophagus

Diaphragm

1 Mouth cavity

*The passage of food through the horse's digestive system. Figures in **bold** indicate the order in which it moves. The liver and spleen are an essential part of the system, although food does not directly pass through them*

The horse eats grass by retracting his lips and cutting with the sharp incisor teeth

The Trickle Effect The horse is a trickle feeder. Effectively this means that there is a continuous intake of food except when resting. Partly digested stomach contents then enter the small intestine continually. Water drunk while the stomach is full tends to travel along the lesser curvature and straight into the duodenum, not mixing with the digesting food. This is potentially a very important happening when considering an organic horse, because the nature and content of this water may have significant influences on digestion. For instance, if excessively acid, it could influence the action of enzymes dependent on an alkaline medium; it could also contribute to acid reflux into the stomach, and the possibility exists that it might irritate and inflame the tissues with which it comes in contact.

WHAT HAPPENS IN THE INTESTINE

The small intestine is the site where, as well as protein, simple sugars and fats are absorbed, and it is these sugars that are a potential source of quick energy. They are abundant in succulent grasses, are available from sugar beet, and are the breakdown product of cereal starches. They are more slowly produced from fat.

Digestion is thus, as becomes clear, a gradual process. Partly digested food enters the large intestine continually too. Some fat is returned to the bowel and further digested in the large intestine. The more complex structural carbohydrates (coming from fibre) are broken down now, helped by the flora of organisms. As is evident from this, there is a constant flow of energy into the bloodstream from different parts of the bowel. It comes from different food sources, is digested in distinctly different ways, and its release for use by the body takes longer for some materials than it does for others. These are factors with a special meaning for the athletic animal.

Absorption from the Bowel This is an essential part of digestion. Breakdown products enter the blood and are taken to the liver, where further breakdown may occur. Complex proteins are broken down into amino acids; carbohydrates are broken into simple sugars, such as glucose; and fats are converted to fatty acids and glycerol. Essentially, fat deposits within the body are the storehouse of energy, to be called up whenever the immediate dietary supply is inadequate. Carbohydrates are used for immediate energy needs, any excess being converted to fat for storage. Protein is essential for tissue-building and replacement.

Excess protein has to be broken down and stored as fat, and this is a wasteful and needless procedure. It places an unnecessary burden on the liver, which is particularly crucial where the liver itself is diseased.

Critical to life is the absorption of all essentials in the correct ratios and balances compatible with need. Remember nature as the perfectionist? This is where the particular demand comes in, and no animal begs perfection more than the racehorse. If the protein is not of adequate quality, the horse will be short of essential amino acids, and the result may be failure of enzyme systems, even within the digestive system. Body structures will then be weakened, leading to disease.

Also, any adverse influence on mineral absorption will result in deficiencies, ultimately leading to illness. This is an everyday problem, and serious because it is less easy to monitor in its early stages than energy and protein deficiency. The horse may not lose condition, energy levels may seem adequate for routine purposes (such as training), and the coat may remain in an acceptable condition; but problems may arise at maximal exertion levels, or the development of growing animals may be imperfect. Calcium and phosphorus are central to this.

Absorption is also affected by inflammation to the bowel, caused either mechanically (through irritant substances, or worms) or by infection. Particular species of worms, at various stages of growth, are plug-feeders, meaning that they eat parts of the bowel lining. These may be present in huge numbers, leaving large areas raw and exposed. Other worms enter the bowel wall and cause irritation and inflammation of the tissues, so interfering with its normal working.

Different types of worms found in horse droppings: (top left) small redworm (cyathostomes); (top right) large redworm (Strongylus vulgaris); (bottom left) tapeworm; (btm right) tapeworm on the caecal wall. Tapeworms are not usually visible in droppings except by microscope

Electrolyte replacement is essential in horses that sweat copiously during arduous events

Use of Energy It is essential for the hungry horse that energy be absorbed soon after ingestion in order to allow life to continue as digestion itself proceeds. Were absorption only to occur from the large bowel, the animal might well expire, under present-day conditions, while waiting for it to happen.

If carbohydrates are not freely available, body fat is used as an energy source until this is depleted; this means that the animal will lose weight, and if this continues, there will ultimately be no energy available for purposes much more vital than movement. An aside here worth mentioning is the question of body heat: horses that are cold burn off energy to produce heat, and may lose condition simply because they are not warm enough. It is a problem of modern management, particularly when clipped horses are kept in cold, damp or draughty conditions.

Calcium and Phosphorus Imbalance In the racehorse, performance-related conditions like tying-up are intimately associated with calcium and phosphorus imbalances – which may result from absorption failure rather than deficiency in the diet. Half the diet's calcium (plentiful in grasses and legumes) is absorbed by the small intestine. It is partly assisted by vitamin D and some proteins. It is inhibited by the fatty acids that form insoluble soaps with calcium, by oxalates (contained in wood sorrel, a grass), by phosphorus levels that are too high, or by bowel disease. It is also, of course, affected by low levels in the diet.

The balance of calcium to phosphorus within the body is critical. Low blood calcium is seen in potentially life-threatening conditions, for example in lactation or long-distance rides, that need immediate treatment. Calcium is lost in sweat, which explains why problems arise in endurance rides. Phosphorus deficiency causes, as well as bone conditions, depraved appetite, stunted growth and infertility. It is a feature of 'bran disease', whereby horses fed largely on bran, or similar foodstuffs, develop symptoms that include lameness and, ultimately, bone changes that may even result in facial and other distortions.

Phytate is a dietary source of phosphorus present in many plants. It can pose problems for horses that do not have the appropriate enzyme (phytase) to digest it. As a result bone formation may be faulty and there will be a disturbed balance of both calcium and phosphorus in the blood.

In the past, phosphorus deficiency in western Europe has been associated with lack of sunlight in stabled animals in winter months (which caused vitamin D deficiency). However, it was common in parts of the USA and Australia, where vitamin D was not in short supply. This occurred because of inhibitors in the grass, a problem that has also occurred in New Zealand.

Other minerals too may be subject to imbalances in a variety of situations, and apparent in the manifestation of other recognised forms of disease. Magnesium is contained in many enzyme systems, most notably those associated with muscle contraction. There is an interaction between calcium and magnesium absorption, as high dietary magnesium can increase calcium uptake, while high phosphorus levels and high oxalates depress magnesium absorption.

Chemical Interference Absorption is also affected by chemicals that interfere with others. As one example, zinc deficiency may result from the over-liming of land; as another, high levels of molybdenum may result in copper deficiency: the end product is disease. Successful management means learning to recognise these situations, and knowing how to take appropriate measures to counter their effects.

An American study has associated human bowel disease with the chlorination of water. Acid water brings the prospect of heavy metals, which are corrosive, and nitrates are believed to cause gastroenteritis and diarrhoea when taken in excessive amounts. All of these create potential absorption problems. The prospect therefore exists that inputs of this nature will adversely affect the working environment of the digestive tract. Absorption is likely to be affected, and a whole range of other problems may ensue.

Food Combinations Digestion may be delayed when combinations of food materials (or other factors, such as nerve degeneration in grass sickness) slow down the normal working of the stomach and intestine. Food transit times are affected by such processes as pelleting and grinding; also they are slower for fibres than for quickly digested, succulent grasses. Alternatively, enzyme failure or the presence of unwelcome chemicals might affect passage time.

It is recognised that the time that material remains in different parts of the tract can vary significantly, even under normal conditions: this is a measure of digestive efficiency. When food is easily digested and presented in simple combinations, the process is at its most efficient and completed in the shortest time. On the other hand, certain other factors can delay digestion, over and above those already mentioned.

Causing Clinical Disease Problems In human dietary writing, the influence of poorly combined food is recognised as a cause of clinical disease problems. In those suffering from stomach and intestinal pain this is seen to exaggerate symptoms, or conversely, to ease them when the practice is stopped. The human, like the horse, is single-stomached, and although our diet is different because we are omnivorous and do not find herbage enticing, there is reason to suspect that digestion time, and food combinations, might have comparable significance for both species.

The problem in man is said to be related to a combination of carbohydrate and protein taken together in a meal. In truth, we do not know enough about this aspect of digestion in the horse. But any factor that delays digestion time will irritate already inflamed tissues, and may well contribute to the inflammation of those that are healthy. The idea has direct benefit to people, like your author, who have suffered from acid indigestion and suspected ulceration. Deliberately avoiding combinations of protein and carbohydrate eases pain, saves energy (because of quicker digestion time) and there is the relief of a lighter stomach. Similarly, simplicity of diet leads to less colic in horses. It might be deducted from this that simple diets are the most sensible. There are many shades of this problem, with origins as diverse as food quality and overloading.

Protein Levels Although modern concentrate feeds tend towards ever higher levels of protein, drawn from a variety of sources, often they are still added to traditional energy constituents, such as oats. We do not know the effect of transit times, and the possible effects on digestion of too much protein. We do know that horses, when introduced to soya bean meal, for example, show signs of gut irritation. From this we must deduce that there is an adverse clinical effect. The long-term significance of this needs to be quantified in relation to overall health and to inflammatory conditions of the bowel. Those who, in years gone by, fed horses on a diet of hay and oats with perhaps only simple additions such as slices of carrot and apple, will say they saw little colic. They also produced recorded performances in competition that have not been significantly bettered, in spite of all the innovations in feeding and training that have since come about. There must be a lesson to be learned from this.

INDIGESTION

Food material that becomes stagnant may decompose and ferment. As already mentioned, mouldy hay causes horses in training to be bloated and unable to perform either at work or in competition. The situation is further complicated by the influence the hay is likely to have on the respiratory system, where it triggers breathing changes, allergies, and often leads to chronic coughing.

Too little fibre, on the other hand, will result in loss of the energy normally derived from large bowel sources. The horse is also likely to show clinical signs in the way of abnormal droppings, be they loose or dry.

Ulcer Formation Ulcers are attributed to excessive and prolonged acidity. They might also be due to the action of local enzymes on exposed tissues; or to failure of the protective mucous coat. But all this is hypothesis. In the human they have been associated with stress, and to emotional and social pressures – neither of which we can sensibly suggest for the horse. Recent medical work has shown that ulcers are caused by bacteria which were previously thought incapable of surviving in such an acid medium as the stomach. The principal organism, *Helicobacter pylori*, is now successfully treated with a combination of drugs; and more recent work has isolated the same organism from ulceration in a horse.

Of course, the question still arises as to whether an organism is capable of causing disease simply by its presence, or if a clinical deterioration of the tissues may occur before infection is possible. It is a question often arising, as inflamed tissues will generally have lost the capacity to protect themselves and may therefore stand open to infection.

FAECES AND THEIR CHARACTER

It has long been recognised that the introduction of new substances to a diet will be reflected by a change in the character of faeces – as we saw earlier. Horses first introduced to even small quantities of soya bean meal, for example, will produce faeces with increased mucus content and which are more fluid; this suggests inflammation, but whether this occurs because the material is in itself irritating, or because the sudden change challenges the ability of the gut to digest it, is unclear. Horses freshly turned out will show signs of grass in the faeces within one to two days. Laxative foods such as bran and sugar beet will make them more liquid. Indigestible materials may make them firm and pelleted.

Any of these changes are simple signs to read. The character of faeces is as good an indicator of digestive health and efficiency as we can get, and changes to their colour and consistency always have to be considered in the light of what is going on within the body. A competition animal whose droppings are too loose might dehydrate; on the

Normal faeces – not too hard, dry or coated with blood or mucus

Loose droppings – may be normal depending on the individual animal and circumstances

Very loose faeces – could be clinically significant in which case the horse might have a temperature, be dehydrated and losing condition

Acute diarrhoea, matting the tail and hair on the legs. Failure to chew results in coarse fibre in the droppings and water retention in the bowel

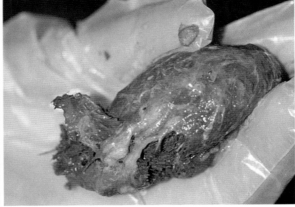

Dropping showing shiny mucus coat, which means the droppings have been slow to pass through the small colon

Heavily mucus-coated faeces as might be observed in cases of colic or bowel inflammation – seen in grass sickness

A high percentage of undigested fibrous material suggests poor mastication and inadequate digestion

Normal faeces with a high fluid content. Watch for signs of dehydration, eg dry coat, lowered performance etc

◀ *Redworm. Small strongyles and large strongyles*

◀ *A dark black colour and 'tarry' consistency suggests bleeding into the higher parts of the gastro-intestinal tract (stomach/ small intestine in particular). This can arise from ulceration or from clotting disorders*

▼ *The make-up of the horse's diet may make the difference between winning and losing*

other hand, if they were too hard, it might already be dehydrated. Then, besides an effect on performance, extremely hard faeces might lead to stoppage and colic. Evident mucus (seen as a sticky outer coating) is a warning that the situation is possibly becoming serious.

WHAT DOES IT ALL MEAN?

For the organic horse, all the above is a guide as to what is ideal, and to what might go wrong as we move to artificial or unnatural feeding. Quite obviously, if we allow the horse to consume irritant substances, the result is anything from discomfort to disease. More seriously for the competing animal, indigestion, problems of absorption, the intake of toxins, all have serious implications for performance. It is not just inflamed tissues and the pain they might cause, but the working of the liver, mineral balances, and the capacity of the circulation to work at the peak efficiency needed. These are all capable of making the difference between winning and losing.

HOW TO ASSIST NATURAL DIGESTION

WHAT YOU CAN DO

1 **Choose** good raw materials (of an organic standard) provided in the right amounts, and keep the diet as simple as possible.

2 **Select** carefully any hay, oats, barley, protein additive, or other supplement.

3 **Inspect** colour, quality and smell; if not wholesome, find an alternative source.

4 **Be critical** about hay and silage quality, especially if your own; if of poor quality, horses may lose condition; if dusty, it may cause respiratory problems.

5 **Protein levels** for growth and development can be as high as 18 per cent, but be wary of any feed that exceeds that; it will be a supplement only.

6 **Levels of protein** for mature horses in full work do not have to exceed those of good oats (10–12 per cent); any excess may produce fat, thereby lowering performance.

7 **Gauge** energy levels against work requirement and bodily condition; many horses will hunt off good hay and silage alone; more breedy types may need concentrates. Energy varies from 7–15 MJ/kg of feed, depending on need.

8 **Provide** adequate roughage and avoid long spells without fibre intake.

9 **Take** any changes gradually to avoid gut disturbance.

10 **Beware** of lush grasses and starch overload.

11 **Always** watch for changes in the faeces and interpret in relation to food intake; distinguish from those caused by sickness.

12 **Provide** a good sloppy mash on a weekly basis, using bran or boiled linseed etc.

13 **Check** the teeth every six months to avoid poor chewing as a result of mouth pain.

14 **Provide** a daily run at clean grass if at all possible.

15 **Avoid** over-complicated feeds except if prescribed for clinical reasons.

16 **Gauge** your horse's physical condition by eye; weighing and measuring may also be helpful.

3 | Organic Ideal and Food Quality

While a true organic horse might be difficult to produce, it is important to assess the standards that might prevent it. Management comes in, as does care of the land and the environment, and it is essential that those who seek a high standard of athleticism in their horse know what is involved. Even if perfection cannot be reached it can be aimed at, and the benefits will be apparent in better and more consistent performance.

Horses in the wild have a variety of food sources, but their nutritional value can be influenced by both nature and man

Definition An organic horse would be one protected fully from adverse effects on growth and disease, and similarly on soundness, longevity and performance. As opposed to organic farming which settles for the attainable, it is necessary to appreciate and exclude all possible adverse influences and to control all daily intakes, especially through food and water. While this standard might not be attainable in a particularly polluted country, it might well be in another that is clean.

What is Organic Food? Organic food for horses would be grown to the same standards as organic production generally, except, perhaps, with more stringent regulation than might be practically possible. The significant difference, if we wish perfection, is control of water quality and to eliminate pollutants that come through the air and on the rain. In this there can be no tolerance of toxins that might cause mineral imbalances, impair liver function, or leave the horse less than fully able to express its athletic ability or be less resistant to infection. It is a matter for the individual owner to be satisfied about source materials, their quality, and whether or not they could be termed – even loosely – 'organic'.

ORGANIC FARMING

The whole organic concept involves a philosophy on environmental principles, on sustainable agriculture, on limiting pollution, maintaining wildlife and supporting the balance of nature in the wild. The standards are set by a variety of controlling authorities in countries or states where organic produce is grown and sold. The International Federation of Organic Agriculture Movements, based in Germany, has member organisations in more than fifty countries. The standards and conditions for growing food and crops, and for producing livestock, avoid the use of artificial fertilisers, synthetic pesticides and weedkillers, and do not allow the use of genetically altered seed or animals.

THE AIMS OF ORGANIC PRODUCTION

It is implicit in the aims of organic production that:
- soil health and fertility be maintained
- there should be high standards of animal welfare
- dependence on non-renewable energy should be minimal
- minimal quantities of fossil fuels should be burned.

Under these standards all inputs to the farming system are controlled and recorded; crop rotations help the control of pests and diseases; and seed sources and dressings are supervised. Standards are rigorously enforced, and when they are not met, punishment is removal of organic accreditation. Feedstuffs for animals are expected to be of an organic standard, and treatments and drugs used have to be recorded.

The idea is that organic farming should coexist with natural biological systems. It should appreciate the significance of natural life in the soil, and the part that organisms play in the cycle of growth and the conversion of energy from the sun into plant materials on which animal and human existence is dependent. These soil organisms can be favoured by the provision of decomposed farmyard waste. Everything in the organic method is aimed at nurturing the soil and producing 'clean' growth that is nutritious and balanced in minerals. It does not preclude dressing with minerals that might be deficient, or of using 'friendly' disease and pest control substances.

THE ROLE OF SOIL ORGANISMS

Not unlike the organisms that digest fibre in the bowel, those in the soil live on the residues of manure and decomposed plant products that are spread on the land, helping to break down non-soluble minerals into salts that are absorbed by the plant roots. They include a myriad of living creatures, ranging from slugs to insects, from bacteria to fungi that invade faeces and help to disperse it.

The consequences of intensive farming often intrude on the health of the living element of the soil, leaving it open to compaction and erosion. This type of farming also causes the depletion of organic matter, the destruction of wildlife habitats, and the pollution of water with leached minerals and other unwanted products – such as herbicides and pesticides – that are indiscriminately shed into general circulation.

The Soil as a Living Element If the soil is a living entity consisting of organisms, minerals and plants, then the whole path of existence is the cyclical conversion of basic elements into complex life, and a constituent part of the organic approach is understanding and respecting this. Concern exists over the drain on natural resources caused by intensive farmland production: the organic answer is through the use of composted manures and other organic matter such as bedding, humus or any natural waste that can be acted upon and will then contribute to further fertility.

It is easy to recognise the existence of a food chain in all this: we know that cattle and sheep eat grass which is converted into meat and milk for our tables. By the same token we can appreciate that the strength and agility of the horse is a product of the energy it consumes through herbage and other crops, and the proteins that build its structure. It is not as simple to recognise that the soil itself is an essential element of this cycle.

How Soil Organisms Work In the simplest terms, soil organisms digest and reduce organic matter, releasing the beneficial elements that it contains, for growth. As an example of this, there are bacteria that live in nodules on the roots of legumes, and which have the ability to fix nitrogen from the atmosphere and make it available for plant nutrition. Similarly, there are small fungal threads that facilitate the transfer of nutrients from soil into the root systems of plants. Soluble artificial fertilisers bypass both of these systems and make the organisms redundant. The possible consequence is excessive levels of nitrates, for instance, in the leaves of plants so affected. This can cause disease in humans and animals.

Essentially, growing plants harbour the energy of the sun to form a store of carbohydrate. These plants will be a protein and energy source for the horse or other consumer, including human, that consumes them. In this they draw nitrogen from the air and take minerals from the ground, and they drink their water from the skies. It is a perfect production plan, until it is polluted.

The Living Population of Soil A wide range of insects, snails and worms makes up the living population of the soil: each has a specific function, and carries out its task in its own specific way. Earthworms, for instance, play an essential part in the aeration and

The purpose of the soil is to convert the energy of the sun into living matter through plant growth

nutrition of the soil, though they cannot survive in acid soils with a pH of less than 5.0. They are also eliminated by the use of chemicals which are toxic to them; these may include artificial fertilisers as well as drugs used in sprays, and perhaps even animal wormers.

All of this varied flora contributes to a means of making food to sustain the lives of those further up the living chain. The plants, working with them, spread roots deep in search of nutrients. They rely on water and on airborne gases, as well as on the energy of the sun, factors which equally influence the growth of organisms; and it may be appreciated that these needs are not dissimilar from the needs of larger beasts.

Soil Types From the viewpoint of our subject, the soil type has little specific effect. We are aware that tradition tells us that horses grow bone best on certain lands – it is thought to be one of the reasons why good horses have always been produced from the limestone lands of Ireland. Peaty bogs have been thought helpful to good foot growth, but the probability is that soft, moist underfoot conditions relieve tenderness and stimulate good horn growth, even in other situations. Some keep horses in deep litter for the same reason, though wet conditions leave horn soft and this does not suit animals being ridden.

Specific soil types are: sands, very light soils, light, medium and heavy soils. The organic matter content increases with clay content. It is lowest in continuous arable conditions and highest in ley-arable systems. The risk of herbicide leaching is greatest on stony or gravelly soils.

Limestone and Minerals The benefit of limestone is in its calcium content, and there is little doubt that horses coming off any kind of deficient land will not grow well and will not have strong bone or hard horn in their feet. The minerals that might affect this growth rate are many, and all it proves is that it is important to know the content in the soil in order to detect any deficiences and to cater for them. The abuse of this kind of knowledge, on the other hand, has many people supplementing their horse's diet with minerals they often do not need. Selenium is an example of this. The problem is not universal, but needs consideration where it exists, whether it is deficient or in excess.

Trace Metals Heavy metals are naturally present in the soil and some are essential, in trace amounts, to animals. Where levels are too high, toxicity is possible, and this needs to be carefully monitored. Zinc, chromium, copper, lead, nickel, cadmium and mercury are all important. Levels that are too high may come from natural conditions, or be caused by environmental pollution of any kind – including local factory emissions – and can even result from inappropriate manuring.

The emissions from these chimneys can affect the soil when brought down via rainfall

The effects of contamination from Chernobyl were widespread. Here are cattle grazing within the danger zone

Calves grazing near Sellafield were seen to have abnormal growths

ORGANIC LIVESTOCK PRODUCTION

A major consideration in animal management under organic systems is care and welfare. There is a depth of meaning in this that cannot be overlooked in dealing with an organic horse; it covers not only the animal's natural physiology, but also its evolutionary development, its behavioural requirements and the design of nature. While recognising the limitations of space posed by domestication as well as the need for housing and feeding, the idea is to stay as close as possible to nature while meeting the basic tenets of Man's needs. It is essential that:

- There should be no over-stocking
- The quality of the grazing should be carefully maintained and managed; parasites, especially, should not be allowed to build up, and there should always be ready access to water
- Animals should be well fed, able to feel free to express their nature, and not be subjected to any avoidable suffering. This would not preclude out-wintering where conditions allowed, although there has to be a practical approach to this – thus a horse straight out of training, suddenly turned out in wet and cold conditions, might well become ill and die. On the other hand another horse that is hardened to the same conditions might not be affected
- Surgical procedures such as castration, essential for behavioural reasons, are not excluded, though unnecessary practices such as nicking and docking would have to be, were they not already illegal. The idea would also preclude embryo transfers and any other routine surgical procedure that was designed to exploit the animal
- In relation to stabling, the requirement would be that horses had adequate space – though having said that, this is not a problem today. It is desirable that all stabled horses be exercised and, where possible, be given a daily run at grass. Of course this is not possible in many establishments, such as many racing yards. Horse feeds would have to be from organic sources. Ideally this would preclude any toxic substance from the environment – we might think of radioactive fallout from the Chernobyl disaster that still remains in parts of Britain. The quality of water would be just as vital, especially when it is accepted that the average US citizen is thought to have traces of at least four toxins in their blood. The question is, how can this be avoided?

> ## CASE NOTE
>
> I once worked for a prominent racehorse trainer whose head lad was giving a 25 per cent protein supplement as a whole feed to the horses. Some were too fat; there was a great deal of muscular lameness; some, already showing signs of impaired liver function from a virus, were blowing unduly after work. With one particular animal, it was necessary to steal the feed from her manger, and replace it with oats: on the supplement, she was stiff and lame; off it, and she won a group race within a few weeks.

The Organic Diet It is important to respect the need for consistency in the diet, and to understand and anticipate the problems of adapting horses to new food materials. But there is no room for deviation from an organic standard, especially as the aim must be to assist the whole development from conception to maturity and rear an animal with all the natural growth and health that nature can provide.

One stipulation in general organic farming regulations is that the diet:

'...should be balanced and of good quality and should not have levels of protein and energy or other additions associated with intensive production.'

This is quoted directly from *The Soil Association Standards for Organic Agriculture*, and it is a very interesting point. Protein levels fed in today's racing establishments and for competition animals are arguably far too high. Excesses, as already mentioned, have to be broken down and converted to fat, and the added burden this places on the liver not only affects efficiency but is an unwanted complication in disease situations.

NEW TRENDS

There are too many innovations and additives in feeding today that are of dubious advantage. For instance, the recent trend of giving oil as an energy source is questionable. Do horses perform any better, and what does it do to their digestive system and to their general physiology? The Soil Association standards prohibit:
'...fats, oils and fatty acids used to produce high protein diets of high nutrient density designed to achieve very early maturity or high levels of production.'

Oils There is no doubt that the very idea of feeding oil is foreign to the animal's nature, as horses could never get food in this way in the wild. That is not to say the bowel cannot deal with oils, but they create a demand for a huge increase in fat-digesting enzymes (lipase); also, some fatty acids form insoluble salts with calcium, so preventing absorption – and how is this answered? Are horses more likely to tie up? We don't know if oils have an effect on pH either in the small or large bowels. The hope is that the energy they provide will be burned off by work. If it is not, the horse will get fat, and the functioning of athletic muscles is likely to be affected if the fat is deposited in them. It is all unanswered, and we shall have to wait and see what it does.

Haylage The recent tendency to use haylage (or ensiled hay), usually sold in large bales, sealed in plastic, has a recognisable appeal. The quality is high, both nutritionally and from the viewpoint of cleanliness and hygiene – but there are hazards: punctured bales are an ideal medium for fungal growth; the same problems as have been found in cattle exist; soil in close-cut silage may contain organisms capable of causing disease. More pertinent, though, as has been seen, is that the presence of dead rats and mice can lead to lethal infection, specifically botulism.

Haylage is generally higher in protein than hay (12–16 per cent dry matter), it has less fibre, and comes in a semi-moist condition that is said to limit the effect of fungal spores. Being fed in a lesser quantity means the horse might have no fibre intake for most of the night. It should also be understood that organisms in the haylage may affect digestion in the same way as they will if present on hay.

Always check the quality of haylage and make sure the bag hasn't been punctured and contains no foreign matter

Yeasts These are fed sometimes in the form of brewer's yeast as a protein and vitamin supplement. It should be appreciated that they are capable of disturbing the gut flora and thereby causing digestive problems.

DIET RESTRICTIONS

The situation for livestock is that:

- 60 per cent of dry matter should consist of fresh green food or unmilled forage produced to organic standards
- Feed brought in from polluted sources should be avoided, such as fishmeal from polluted sea waters . Any food of animal origins – which directly offends the horse's natural digestion – could not be fed in an organic diet
- Farming standards restrict the use of commercially produced compounded feeds
- They prohibit any food containing antibiotic residues
- Mineral and vitamin supplementation is only allowed where there is evidence of a deficiency on soil or blood analysis. But it is interesting to note, however, that the following are permitted: seaweed, rock salt, yeast, di-calcium phosphate, cod liver oil, wheat germ, limestone/ chalk flour, calcined magnesite and vitamin D
- Concentrated vitamins and pure amino acids are restricted, though the specific demands of intensive training do create a need for vitamins such as folic acid, biotin, vitamin B12, that need to be replaced. However, there is a tendency for this kind of supplementation to be carried too far, and over-use of substances such as vitamin C and vitamin E is common, where answers might more appropriately be found in better understanding of the disease problems being observed. Vitamin C only protects against infection where it is deficient; and vitamin E is a paltry contributor to the solving of muscular or reproductive problems generally
- There must be no synthetic products fed – no kind of growth promoter, antibiotic or probiotic, except for purely therapeutic reasons

 *Health is reflected in body condition and the shine of the coat*

Maintaining Good Health It is central to this idea that '...animals should be sustained in good health by effective management practices, including high standards for animal welfare, appropriate diets and good stockmanship rather than relying on veterinary medication'. The same would apply to the organic horse: 'Health in farm animals is not simply the absence of disease, but also the ability to resist infection, parasitic attack and metabolic disorders, as well as the ability to overcome injury by rapid healing.'   This is the very essence of what we are looking for. Illness, of course, has to be treated, but the aim is to complement the natural healing processes rather than simply to treat symptoms and trust that this will work. In other words, where a horse gets an infection – say, pneumonia – treatment would not just consist of an antibiotic: it is important to maintain an adequate dietary intake (this might have to be stomach-tubed or drip-fed in extreme cases), and to ensure that the environment helps recovery. The horse must be kept warm enough, and free from draught and dampness, yet he must get adequate fresh air. These are factors that directly affect natural disease resistance – they are common sense. Sunshine and grass are a natural benefit where this can be arranged. Above all, the horse must have the treatment it needs to ensure recovery – as we can see, more than simply a matter of medication.

Preventive Measures Preventive medicines are only permitted where there is a known problem, but the situation for the horse might be significantly different from farm animals. It still has to be decided if the recurring infections we see are a consequence of management practices – as is virtually certain. If so, then prevention might be best helped by recognition of this and by taking appropriate steps to counter it. But protection against viruses like flu would have to stay until a day could be envisaged when universal standards made them unnecessary, or, at least, their prevention could be seen in a different light.

Worm Control 'The control of intestinal worms must be achieved primarily by good livestock management practices, and where appropriate, optimum stocking rates, rotational grazing, clean grazing systems and mixed stocking.'

Where there is a problem, control by non-chemical means should be applied and this monitored by regular faecal examination. In horse management, this might well only be possible by physically removing faeces from the field under intensive conditions. Grazing rotation with other species of animal might also help, but there are worms that exploit this situation. Anthelminthic drugs are only used where unavoidable and treatment is not repeated. The need for future use is avoided. Such problems naturally beg the questioning of stocking rates and other matters of management, such as paddock resting and crop rotations. They are not easily answered by an owner whose horse has to live, browse, eat and sleep in a back garden.

Specifically prohibited for cattle are products that interfere with the normal breakdown of dung and damage the flora and fauna of the soil – the avermectins, in particular (which poses a particular problem for horse worm dosing). Organophosphorus and organochlorine compounds are also prohibited. This is taken so seriously that where organophosphates are used, animals compulsorily treated under statutory conditions will lose their organic status fully for meat purposes, and dairy animals will have

The higher the stocking rates the greater the risk of worms

to undergo a conversion period before their milk can be used again. As a consequence it must be asked if there are health and performance implications for horses dosed with these drugs when in full training.

Nitrates and their Management It is appropriate here to take as an example the part played by nitrogen in plant feeding, and the way its improper management can pose disease problems for animals and Man. Nitrogen is a vital constituent of proteins and amino acids, and so it is present in all living cells. It is especially important to the growth of plants, through which the grazing horse obtains its nitrogen, and is the most common constituent of grassland fertilisers. Artificial nitrogenous fertilisers contain soluble nitrogen that may leach into waterways and is capable of causing pollution. These also have an adverse effect on long-term fertility of soil, on the nutritional quality of the crops they are used on, and on the organic matter that is the essential living element of the soil.

There is an on-going debate about the toxicity of nitrate in water for both humans and animals exposed to it. While there are distinct pathological pathways, the extent to which they might affect the disease status and performance potential of horses is unknown. What is known, however, is that nitrates cause human gastroenteritis when taken in large quantities, but more importantly, they are a possible source of toxic nitrites. While there is no research that associates equine gastroenteritis with nitrate intake, it is not unusual to encounter horses with blue surface membranes and shortness of breath at exercise, symptoms which are considered to be typical of nitrite poisoning. These are also symptoms, admittedly, that might be due to other causes: in cattle, for instance, the excessive concentration of nitrate in green beet or turnip tops can lead to a known type of toxicity. Nitrates can be found even in hay, and in numerous other food materials.

Inevitably, in an athletic animal, any degree of nitrite poisoning would affect performance, because it reduces the blood's capacity to transport oxygen to the tissues. It can be very serious when it happens.

▼ Seepage from farmyard manure heaps may contaminate water courses. Innocent-looking water like this might contain unwanted chemicals – and there is a risk of liver fluke from the grasses at the edges

CASE NOTE

In the particular instance referred to here, the condition was not a simple case of nitrite toxicity, and there were other expressions of disease. But it was impossible to prove that unidentified chemicals in the water supply were not adding to the effect of the nitrate. Either way, the trainer was never able to train his horses. They suffered varied and repeated problems over a number of years, for which there was no logical answer other than water-borne toxicity. Every single aspect of management and diet was fully assessed. The horses would come in well from grass, be trained to a state of fitness that made it possible to undertake fast work, perhaps even get to racing. Then, inexplicably, their condition melted away, they showed advanced signs of muscular lameness, and most of them tied up. Frequently they blew excessively after work and their membranes were blue in appearance. Laboratory analysis revealed a mineral deficiency, but feeding the required minerals didn't cure the problem. Over a time, all sorts of remedies were tried, but without success. Eventually the trainer simply gave up, but there was little other than water-borne toxins to explain the problem, even despite filtering to reduce the water's nitrate content after which the blue membranes and shortness of breath were reduced.

AN ORGANIC SYSTEM FOR HORSES

While the aims of organic farming generally are practical as well as idealistic, the most basic need in a system for horses is to ensure nutritional quality throughout life. This includes the elimination of toxic substances from any source, and to achieve mineral and vitamin levels to provide balanced growth and development. The normal functioning of disease resistance systems is naturally implied; as well as the expression of ability and performance to the peak of its potential for the individual animal.

Allowing a Natural Life An important principle is that animals should live a natural life, close to that designed by nature. Today, their freedom to roam is impeded by hedgerows, ditches and fences, but limited restrictions of that type do not exclude natural expression. As paddocks get smaller, however, to a state where horses may live virtually their whole lives confined to stables, then life quality is affected. Those who control them then have a duty to ensure this does not lead to disease, shorten life expectancy, or impose standards of welfare that might be capable of being termed 'cruel'.

We seldom now permit stallions to run loose with their mares. We break, ride, drive and use horses for a complex of purposes not necessarily designed by nature, though we try to do it in a way that is free from excessive discipline and that gainfully employs the natural instincts and talents of the individual animal. Thus horse racing is successful not only because horses are willing and obedient, but because the element of competition is in their nature; in their natural state the dominant, quickest and strongest stallion being the one who gets the mares. He can fight and outrun his opponents, and he has an instinct to implant his offspring in the best-looking stock. Their foals will race and gambol in the open air.

Eliminating Intensive Production

It is a primary aim of organic farming to eliminate intensive livestock production, especially where commercialism oversteps animal welfare. This is where disease becomes an accounted statistic, and death is measured in percentages that only relate to the financial health of the operation. Sadly, this has been a feature of horse breeding over recent years. Racing, too, has tended towards an increase in numbers per training unit. It has to be asked what the effects of this are on the individual animal, specifically on its comfort and well-being, and on its life expectancy. The point comes home most bluntly when we consider the somewhat ludicrous recent effort to fit nappies, or diapers, to horses in order to (mostly) save labour.

Producing Clean Food

It has been found in research that organically produced food has higher dry matter and vitamin contents and also better storage qualities. These are serious considerations in horse feeding if they favour the development of normal, strong, healthy bone that will not be subject to fractures or conditions such as rickets or OCD (a disease of joint cartilage and underlying bone); and if they provide the means to disease resistance and to the avoidance of conditions that might adversely affect performance, such as tying up.

At the very least we will take organic food to mean food that is clean of all traces of pesticide, artificial fertiliser or herbicide, and grown in ways that enhance nutritional quality by natural means. Ultimately, the full attainment of organic standards has to begin with a gradual removal of pollutants, and this necessarily begins with those under direct control. In the longer term it is increasingly recognised that measures need to be taken to return the Earth's atmosphere to a standard consistent with that designed by nature. If this is not achievable, only those capable of surviving a new challenge would be able to continue living. Those, both human and animal, unable to withstand the influences of bad water, polluted food and impure air, would naturally die off. Others who can show resistance might carry on, but at what cost and in what state of health?

In the end, a horse with weakened bone will not be of use as a riding animal. One with constant infection will become untrainable; and if there is a continued growth, however small, in the incidence of digestive diseases – even simple indigestion – performance will be less attainable. Competitive equine sport will fall apart if our horses are unwell, and this is an outlook that will grow increasingly real if it is ignored. By accepting the prospect, we are, at least, starting to do something about it.

Health in the wild may be affected by environmental conditions. In a controlled organic system the aim is to promote vigour and eliminate disease as depicted by this stallion and his mares in Patagonia (top) and these Lusitano stallions fighting in Portugal (bottom)

AIMING FOR ORGANIC FOOD STANDARDS

WHAT YOU CAN DO

1 **If you depend** on buying all your feed, find a supplier who will provide the quality you want; remember any organic food has to meet set standards of production.

2 **If buying** oats, for example, make sure they look good to the eye, are hard and clean and full-bodied; ascertain the protein level and energy value.

3 **Try to learn** the origin and, if possible, buy oats that are free from artificial fertilisers or sprays, and have been saved without rain – that is, not dusty, musty or shrivelled.

4 **Aim to ensure** that the land your horses run on, and that their food is produced from, is kept to organic standards.

5 **Do not feed** freshly harvested, inadequately dried, or poorly stored grains, or any that have been sprayed in storage.

6 **Be careful** in buying nuts or material where the contents are unclear – the sweepings of oats from an empty grain loft can contain as much as 10 per cent protein.

7 **Be scrupulous** in buying hay and ensure it has adequate digestible fibre, is of a known feeding value and contains a balanced mineral content.

8 **Hay or silage** off deficient land may itself be deficient.

9 **It is critical** that hay should be clean to the eye and nose; spores may smell sweet and do not have to cause discoloration; suspect any that is discoloured.

10 **Look for** hay saved without rain; in wet years this might mean buying the previous year's hay; do not feed fresh hay until properly seasoned.

11 **Do not use** silage bales where the bags have been perforated and discard any that contain the remains of any dead creature such as a rodent.

12 **Do not use** silage that is discoloured, that smells unwholesome, or evidently contains fungi.

13 **When buying** hay or silage always seek a nutritional breakdown – which may mean having a sample sent for analysis – in order to avoid deficiencies.

14 **Do not keep** horses intensively and try to provide a quality of life that allows a degree of natural expression.

4 Feed Additives and Supplements

Ballière's *Comprehensive Veterinary Dictionary* defines 'feed additive' as: 'material added to the food of animals with an express purpose of effecting a change in the well-being or composition of the animal and likely to affect its biological functions...' It describes 'feed supplement' as: 'nutritive materials which are feedstuffs in their own right and which are added to a basic diet such as pasture to supplement its deficiencies. Includes trace elements and macrofeeds such as protein supplements.'

It needs to be stated that the current horse-owning population is being assailed with such a variety of additives and supplements that logic has been lost, and it must be suspected that commercial gain has more to do with this than the benefit of the horse. There seems to be a 'chaos theory' in operation – the more information that is thrown at the public the more confusion will be created – and it might be admitted that science contributes to this.

When papers are published relating to research projects, they are often the bullets to be fired at the unwitting in this war between manufacturers and consumers – and little time is devoted to feeling concered about the horse! As an example: it has long been known that vitamin E plays a part in reproductive function and in the prevention of muscular dystrophy. Research in the seventies into selenium deficiency – a mineral that operates in conjunction with vitamin E – led to an awareness that particular geographical areas were deficient. As both reproductive failure and birth defects in foals occur where these two substances are in inadequate supply, a minor panic spread through the horse world, the upshot being that everyone thought they were in a deficient area! The range of symptoms reported was, however, diverse and often imagined

PROPER USE OF SUPPLEMENTS

- Feed a balanced ration and do not be influenced by fashion.
- Be objective about publicity relating to vitamins, minerals, protein, energy and oils.
- Only supplement where there is good reason to suspect deficiency.
- Know the mineral status of your own soil and food produce, including hay and silage; then make necessary additions.
- Be careful about multiple supplements, as toxicity is possible.
- Horses produce B vitamins in the bowel, but amounts may prove inadequate for heavy exercise.
- Green grass is the most natural whole food source, but quality varies with the area and the season.
- Foals often need supplementary calcium.

– yet still providers found it profitable to sell feeds rich in vitamin E and selenium. And even now, veterinary surgeons prescribe them as the solution to all sorts of muscular conditions not even remotely related to muscular dystrophy. Objectively the situation would appear to be 'over the top', and while deficiencies can and do occur, the incidence would appear to be low, except in specific and detectable situations. Most diets containing cereals and green plants have plenty of vitamin E in them. We are told that vitamin E is an anti-oxidant and essential in infectious disease resistance. But enough is all that is needed, and where there is already plenty, infections are not going to benefit from supplementation. The same applies to selenium, except in the specifically deficient areas: there is no benefit from feeding it unless it is lacking. The same also applies to other vitamins and minerals.

No one will dispute that our civilisation has saved the horse from the risk of extinction. Without a part to play in our lives, it might not have survived in the wild and would have been as vulnerable as other species which are challenged. Yet the benefits of man's patronage are sometimes a challenge to its very nature, as we have seen: the original horse was not going to find a feed of peas or beans, nor was it going to drink a pint of oil anywhere in the open ranges; nor, of course, was it ever going to be fitted with shoes, or saddles, or draw heavy drays – so it was its usefulness to society, in reality, that saved it. And it is here that its natural requirements are often compromised to fit its life as a domesticated servant.

In shoeing horses, the need for which is not disputed, we are simply recognising a problem and answering it in the only way possible. However, in filling the horse's gut with challenging nutrients, more thought needs to be given to the side-effects.

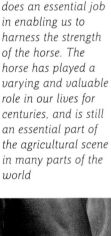

The farrier does an essential job in enabling us to harness the strength of the horse. The horse has played a varying and valuable role in our lives for centuries, and is still an essential part of the agricultural scene in many parts of the world

A Clean Gut

One potential problem recognised is the accumulation of dirt in the large bowel. The practice of purging (or physicking) horses was routine, and as common as it was to give children senna pods, cascara or spoonfuls of 'Andrews' Liver Salts'. Contemporary wisdom holds that purging horses is outdated, and the logic of it is either questioned or disapproved of. Yet those of us who routinely purged horses twenty years ago can attest to the benefits, and also to the frequently seen symptoms that were considered to indicate the need for it. The problem is caused by the ingestion of dust and dirt, soil, sand, and any material that might sediment on the bottom of the bowel and act as a foreign, unmoving mass there.

Affected horses are not ill, but they are useless for racing or competition, having little energy and never progressing in their training. Usually their coats are dull, they are pot-bellied, their legs fill, and the very manner in which they respond to purging leads to a feeling that routine measures should be adopted to prevent the condition. In the past, trainers had their own time and method for physicking their horses; thus they all might have been treated when they came up from grass, or when they went out, or both. Some Flat trainers did all their horses at Christmas, giving them a break for a few days: thus doses were given and consumed in the feed, the horses purged about twenty-four hours later, and then dried up again within another twenty-four. Few, if any, ever showed an adverse reaction, and most showed a benefit.

Free range horses like this pony on Dartmoor may be able to browse on cleaner land than those living near to developed industrial areas

While it has to be accepted that purging may intrude on the well-being of the bowel organisms, volumes of indigestible material will hardly benefit them either. Many owners still purge their horses with anything from linseed oil to Epsom salts. In the wild it is possible that cascara, extracted from the bark of the Californian buckthorn, would have the same effect, or senna pods, eaten from the shrub on which they grow.

Some Feeding Pointers

- The correct level of dietary protein is 8–12 per cent, the higher levels for growth and development.
- Grass is a good natural source.
- Good oats were the basis of horse diets in the past, for work and sport, though some types cannot deal with the energy. They are high in phosphorus.
- Beware of the effects of dietary oils, as they may cause absorption problems and mineral imbalances.

The reason for mentioning this here is because the basis of good nutrition is a clean and healthy gut, functioning effectively to break down eaten food and absorb its essential value for the use of the body. Anything that affects absorption, as we know, will intrude on this, and may lead to imbalances, deficiencies, illness and perhaps even death. With a clean gut, and a worm-free one too, the horse can make best use of its food.

Without this essential it will fail to thrive, and nowadays this often leads to the feeding of all sorts of additives and supplements: minerals and vitamins are poured in, protein is increased, starches are added and varied. Yet improvement may still be hard to identify, so another source is added, and so it continues. However, in order to perform at peak efficiency, the horse only needs an adequate intake of protein, carbohydrate and fat; it does need vitamins, minerals and trace elements, but in the right amounts and the correct proportions. (It also needs to be free of infection and lameness, naturally.) All these dietary elements should be acquired in a digestible form and be absorbed in the correct balances, and all should be available from good quality basic feeds. The proof of the pudding is in the eating, they say, and the fact that horses peformed as well in the past on simpler diets must make us question what we are trying to do today.

MINERAL IMBALANCE

- Mineral imbalances may occur because of soil deficiency.
- They may be precipitated by absorption problems.
- Dietary influences may be a factor, such as excessive bran.
- Excessive liming can cause problems.
- Environmental factors, including water quality, are important.

FACTORS AFFECTING CONDITION AND PERFORMANCE

Deficiencies of protein, carbohydrate and fat are simple to evaluate. Thus underfed horses are short of energy and poor in condition, and the cause of the problem is in the quantity and quality of the food. Specific vitamin and mineral deficiency conditions, on the other hand, occur either because the food is directly deficient, or because some external factor affects availability or absorption. A recognised example of this is the interplay between molybdenum and copper, whereby an excess of one may cause a deficiency of the other. The horse world is well informed of the significance. Specific diagnosis is made by blood analysis and food assessment, and sometimes by soil and herbage evaluation. The symptoms are often indicative – though it must be said, if the deficiency is marginal, it may go unnoticed.

Real signs may only be expressed in animals that are pushed to the limit of performance; then the subclinical effect merges with the scenario called 'poor performance syndrome', a contrived title for a complex of very specific conditions. In the main, horses perform below par either because of lameness, which is possibly even more common than in human athletes, or because one or more of a multiplicity of conditions has affected the normal working of the body tissues; this latter may arise through inflammation of lung tissue, or it could occur from conditions as uncomplicated as anaemia, or mineral imbalances, or poisonings. What must be made clear is that each condition is specific and capable of diagnosis, and usually treatment; the idea that there

▲ *The quality of the mare's milk may influence foal deficiencies*

is a mysterious and impenetrable syndrome that cannot be deciphered is anything but realistic. It is also important to appreciate that minor deficiencies of even trace elements can be critical in animals that have to compete or race.

SPECIFIC DEFICIENCIES

Details of deficiencies can be found in a variety of books. Here we will only consider the organic horse, firstly its requirements regarding a full complement of all essentials, and also the situations which are likely to leave it short.

A diet of good oats, hay, and an hour or two at grass, will provide all a horse wants in the way of nutrients. Problems arise when the quality is not good. Poorly produced, or saved, oats may be low in protein, energy and mineral levels. Good oats, however, are high in phosphorus as compared to calcium (which is not beneficial, especially to the growing horse, and needs to be balanced out); they also contain potassium, lysine and B vitamins. The unsuitable calcium/phosphorus ratio can be significant if there is not a good alternative source of calcium in the diet, although this is balanced partly by hay, and further by grass, especially in the presence of clovers (but tread carefully here, because growing clovers are not well tolerated by laminitic animals).

There is a case to be made for supplementing calcium to young growing horses, especially foals, and particularly when the quality of the dam's milk is falling off and the autumn paddocks are hard and bare. Epiphyseal enlargements are common at this time, seen at the knee and fetlock joints. Such swellings should not be ignored, because irreparable damage can be done and permanent limb deformities may ensue. If necessary, calcium can be added as dicalcium phosphate to a simple diet as described above, or a variety of vitamin/mineral mixtures is available on the market to guard against possible deficiency.

ELECTROLYTES

It is sensible to supplement any mineral if there is an indication of deficiency, but the cause must be identified and the supplementation should be specific. Deficiencies of sodium, chloride and potassium do occur, as a result, among other reasons, of losses incurred through sweating in exercise. They are routinely replaced in the form of balanced electrolyte preparations, and there is a wide variety on the market. It should be appreciated that these vary greatly in effectiveness. Electrolytes prepared for other species are usually not suitable for horses, and some preparations give better results than others. The measure of success is in the response from the animal, as dehydrated horses have dry, tight coats, they tend to become progressively lighter in condition, and eventually lose form. Electrolytes that are effective will prevent this happening. However, these symptoms might also result from low-grade infections, in which case no kind of electrolyte will cure the problem. The message is therefore be sure of the diagnosis, otherwise a great deal of waste will occur.

It has long been customary to provide salt as a lick or as common salt (at about 2oz per day) in the feed. This was done because of the loss of salt in sweat, and it was also believed that the horse was innately in need of added salt. Mares at stud responded to intra-uterine infusions of salt, used to stimulate reproductive cycling; horses in training were drenched with saline washes. However, with the advent of well balanced electrolytes, most of this has been discontinued. Uterine function is seen in a different light – though it could be suggested that dehydrated mares, and especially those straight out of training, do not produce fertile follicles without some help. Sea salt is a source of iodine, and is used in iodine deficiency, but it is dangerous to supplement without knowing the precise nutritional status. Iodine deficiency can lead to enlarged thyroid glands (seen at the top of the jugular furrow on either side of the neck), but enlarged glands may also occur where there is an excess, in which case added iodine will only exacerbate the problem. Blood tests will help clarify the situation, and soil and herbage analysis will show if an excess of another mineral might be affecting availability: too much liming (high in calcium), for example, can affect zinc availability. Therefore cause and effect need to be known to resolve any problem.

By and large, it should be adequate to provide electrolytes whenever a horse

Essential minerals are lost in sweating and need to be replaced to prevent imbalance

sweats during or after exercise. Modern practice tends to be exceptionally liberal in this regard, and really just once or twice a week should be enough during training, as there will be a continual supply of the same minerals from the diet anyway. Properly balanced electrolytes enter the bloodstream quickly and help to restore fluid levels lost through dehydration, and the effects are reflected in the general condition of the animal as well as its performance at work.

TRACE ELEMENTS

Clinical trace element deficiencies occur under particular conditions, for instance whenever there is a deficiency in the soil or herbage. In such cases, symptoms are seen in grazing animals, and may include anything from colour changes in the hair to hoof deformities, and bone and teeth abnormalities. The problem may be caused by absolute deficiency, by excess or imbalance of other elements, or by failure of absorption from the gut.

(below left) Horn health is affected by biotin deficiency as shown, where poorer quality horn can be seen above the darker,

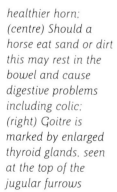
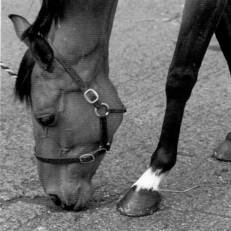

healthier horn; (centre) Should a horse eat sand or dirt this may rest in the bowel and cause digestive problems including colic; (right) Goitre is marked by enlarged thyroid glands, seen at the top of the jugular furrows

There is always a reason when horses are poor and unthrifty. If it is not obvious, it may be necessary to have a full clinical evaluation, including blood and soil samples. Besides loss of condition, there can be infertility, skin conditions, and birth defects in foals; in horses in full training, there may be problems with performance.

Where there is poisoning, the source must be found. However, land polluted by factory effluents (or even by radioactive fallout) needs to be monitored before it can again become usable for animal production.

TYING UP

This is a problem seen particularly in racehorses today: those in full work are affected, and suffer varying degrees of muscular seizure. Originally called 'Monday morning disease', it occurred in draught horses in heavy work after they were rested on Sundays without their rations being reduced – they stiffened when they went out, and the condition could be so severe that they were unable to move and even passed bloody urine.

While this is well understood now, and does not need to be a recurring problem, other expressions of the same condition are seen and can be difficult to overcome. The modern fashion is for blood analysis, and this shows increased muscle enzyme levels. Research relates some occurrences to disturbances of mineral metabolism, but there are other causes too: the condition is common in chronically infected animals, in those kept in cold conditions, and on particular types of diet; thus some horses tie up on barley, and others on high protein supplements. There is generally a specific reason, and the logical approach is to find and correct it – not to pour in minerals and vitamins in the hope of overcoming the effect.

Tying up also occurs, as was mentioned earlier, when external factors (as in the Case Note in the last chapter) affect mineralisation. Whether these affect absorption or not needs to be proven. We also need to know what the specific factors are: for instance, are they many and diverse? Are some influenced by toxins carried in water? Or do they prevail on the land as a result of rainfall or imbalances created in herbage?

INCREASED DEMAND

Various activities increase the volume of minerals and vitamins needed by the body, as in lactation, pregnancy, growth and work. Work is possibly the least investigated of these, but modern research has supported the view, long held, that vitamins such as folic acid and vitamin B12 can become deficient in highly trained horses and need supplementation. It is suggested that this may occur through the effect of adrenalin release on gut organisms, and thus vitamin production in the large bowel. Supplementation needs to be done with care, however, and it may be that an hour at grass will have more benefit than anything added to the feed. The work explains why the response to vitamin injections given to racehorses is effective, despite age-old academic assurances that production in the large bowel made it unnecessary.

The more dramatic effects of mineral deficiencies are seen in conditions such as milk fever and 'diaphragmatic flutter', already mentioned. The latter is more likely to occur in warmer weather and is marked by collapse, respiratory distress and a thumping sound from the diaphragm. It is treated intravenously on the spot, otherwise the horse might die.

Osteochondrosis dissecans (OCD) is a lameness condition of mostly developing horses; it is causing concern in professional circles because it appears to be on the increase. Professor Jeffcott, in a paper presented to the British Equine Veterinary Association at Cambridge in 1991, mentioned an '... apparently escalating incidence and enormous losses caused to racing, breeding and equestrian competition'. There is some suggestion that it is a disease caused by management practices, and numerous scientific projects align its development to diet: feeds too rich in carbohydrate and protein are blamed, and disturbances of the calcium and phosphorus metabolism; there is also thought to be an association with copper deficiency. Its cause is associated with efforts to push the growth and development of young horses.

The lesson to be drawn from all this is that diets causing this condition are not suitable for the production of an organic animal, as they do not comply with the natural demands of healthy growth and development. They involve using protein and energy ingestion to the limits, and this is intensive production – and as such it is incompatible with the organic ideal. There is also no hard evidence that such diets improve performance. It makes no sense continually to increase protein levels, as the surplus simply presents the body with added work in dealing with it. Likewise, obliging the animal to handle large quantities of concentrated fats is a move as far away from Nature as it is possible to go.

HERBAL PRODUCTS

There is a wide selection of herbal substances used for preventive and therapeutic purposes in contemporary equine medicine. Some have transferred from human medicine, and some have long been used in the horse world. It has to be seen that much of this use is empirical, and much of it is without any great degree of logic.

In any disease condition, precise diagnosis is important. Simply because a horse has laboured breathing after exercise doesn't mean there is one simple cause that can be resolved by any substance acting on the respiratory system. If the cause is a bacterial infection, the most effective treatment is a suitable antibiotic. If it is due to a mineral imbalance, then the obvious measure is to correct it. On the other hand, if there is respiratory mucus but without infection, the problem may be relieved by any substance that will expel it from the lungs. (Note that drugs such as corticosteroids, for example, used extensively in conventional medicine to reduce lung inflammation without

▼ *Natural healers: (top)* Salix babylonica, *original source of aspirin and (bottom)* Atropa belladonna, *source of atropine*

eliminating the cause, are ill-advised and potentially dangerous. It is vital to identify the cause, and to relieve it, otherwise irreparable harm can be done.)

Many therapeutic substances are condemned through misuse, others become over-used, and all of this simply because this field is complex and often misread. It is an area into which drugs, supplements and additives are thrown blindly in the hope that they will work – although frequently they do not. Where they appear to, the reason an animal recovers may have nothing to do with treatment: there is far too much commercial intrusion here, and far too much poor medical practice. No therapeutic substance can be a cure-all, covering every condition from head-shaking to tail-scratching – in fact, the more conditions a remedy is said to cure, the more there is reason to be wary. However, herbal medicine is, in fact, the root source of a great deal of modern pharmacology. It is also a field likely to expand greatly in the future as intensive research into exotic plants and organisms is undertaken. In the southern Mexican state of Chiapas, for example, work being carried out promises to unravel secrets known to the isolated Mayan people for centuries. They use a variety of herbal substances which have not been researched, and some of which they have used successfully in human diseases.

Aspirin, as is well known, was originally extracted from willow bark; atropine, used principally for its actions on the respiratory system, came from deadly nightshade. There are old herbalists in existence who use extracts of unspecified plant roots for conditions in horses. Some of these have a particular effect and are beneficial. However, it is at the heart of our progress today that such products must be based on analysis, research and understanding: only in that way can we separate the good from the bad and refine the beneficial products so they can be used in specific situations where they are likely to help. Using natural products is compatible with the ideals of an organic horse. But the basis is precise knowledge, and not the blind principles that at present often pertain.

Our knowledge is often primitive, despite the last century of research and discovery, and the essence of any future has got to be with understanding. The advantage of science is its ability to find active ingredients, and to purify and enhance them. The advantage of medicine should be specific diagnosis, thus ensuring that the cause is found, and that the correct substance is used in treatment, with effect. Throwing blanket treatments at horses for undiagnosed and misunderstood conditions only leads to chronic illness and frustration. Extracts of the mountain tobacco plant, for instance, may soothe wounds and bruises, but taken internally it does not cure diseases of unknown cause. This is a lesson we must learn. There needs to be an infusion of common sense into horse therapy, because however frustrated owners may become with the shortcomings of veterinary medicine, the path forward is not in empirical ideas but in wisdom. That is not to deny veterinary medicine is headed down a dark alley, leaning too heavily on technology. But the answer to clinical conditions is best found in conventional traditions, perhaps requiring a new accent on human observation rather than reliance on machines. The answers are there facing us, if only we would look: indeed, they are mostly just common sense.

HOMOEOPATHY

This is a system of treatments founded by Samuel Hahnemann (1755–1843), a German doctor and chemist. His idea was to treat diseases with minute amounts of substances capable of causing the same symptoms in healthy animals. While the principles are not proven, homoeopathy has a considerable following today – though whether this stems from the failings of conventional medicine or the benefits of the therapy is often unclear. The effective treatment of diseases is based on diagnosis, the removal of precipitating factors, and through helping the natural resistance mechanisms to restore functional normality.

A horse fed an improper diet may have all sorts of digestive problems, and symptoms, but the answer is to correct the diet, not to impose treatment on it. Successful homoeopathic treatments deserve research and evaluation. However, it is a form of therapy as much abused by its practitioners as any other form of medicine, simply because blanket cures do not exist. Tablets for back pain will not do much for animals that need manipulation or physiotherapy; the idea that they might stimulate natural immunity cannot hold water where the problem does not involve the immune system.

NUTRACEUTICAL MEDICINE

On the basis that conditions such as asthma and eczema have strong dietary influences, nutraceutical medicine (a recent US interest) uses naturally derived substances to promote normal body functions. What effectively is involved is the influence on body systems of food quality, and the availability of its elementary constituents for use. In other words it is an organic concept, fostering the removal of harmful contents, and making minerals and vitamins available as they are required for normal growth and development, for disease resistance and the repair of damaged tissues. There is nothing here that is alien to us: at its heart is information like that relating to folic acid and vitamin B12 in racehorses, critical information that can lead to correction and so foster the whole needs of the athletic horse.

There is, of course, a need to balance this, and not follow the common tendency to go overboard with it. Transferring research from the human field can prove counterproductive. The horse needs enough of what is necessary, and imbalances created by over-supplementation lead to as many problems as a deficiency. This premise applies to a number of dietary supplements that have become available for arthritic conditions and joint repair; among these are glucosamine, chondroitin, commercially produced collagen from chicken carcases, and shark cartilage. Such preparations are being widely used for joint conditions and the repair of tissues, such as tendons and cartilage, that are collagenous (collagen is a structural protein): in other words, they have a specific physiological basis, and they are not miracle cures for all conditions involving these tissues. Where there is no pathology, there is no need for supplementation.

From an organic viewpoint, the message is that enough is as good as a feast, and over-supplementation can cause problems that didn't previously exist. The value of a natural, organic diet (including fresh grass), balanced to the animal's needs and not fed to excess, is that vitamin and mineral levels can be expected to be adequate, with perhaps some supplementation to cover the excessive demand for B vitamins in trained horses, also electrolytes, and allowance for any excesses or deficiencies peculiar to the locality. Remember, the presence of toxins of any kind may affect availability or absorption, and it is impossible to evaluate these risks from most commercial food sources. But the discovery of clinical signs only means the exact cause needs to be unearthed, not a whole range of products fed to further confuse the situation.

NATURAL SUBSTANCES AFFECT HEALTH

Vegetable oils play a part in the treatment of skin diseases: in their role as natural hormone precursors, they influence tissue repair, arthritic conditions and blood mechanisms. However, that is not to say that they might prove to be of benefit when used to excess.

Anti-oxidants are epitomised by substances such as vitamins C and E; they play a part in the body's defences against infection, and in dealing with toxins of plant and environmental origin. Powerful sources are green grasses, and sun-ripened fruit and vegetables. They are particularly important in helping recovery from illness.

UNDERSTANDING ADDITIVES AND SUPPLEMENTS

WHAT YOU CAN DO

1 **The need** for these has to be measured against physical condition, food quality (including grazing) and demands of work.

2 **Deficiencies** arise through deficient inputs, through deficient grazing land, or through the ingestion of chemicals, minerals or organisms that affect absorption.

3 **If the diet** is adequate and the animal is not holding condition, clinical tests, like blood tests, are needed to detect underlying disease or point to possible absorption problems.

4 **Food,** herbage and soil analysis may be required to supplement these.

5 **For horses in heavy work,** vitamin and mineral supplementation may be essential to help hold condition as well as to perform; take advice if in doubt.

6 **Electrolyte loss** from exercise and sweating may not be adequately replaced from normal dietary sources and a balanced electrolyte mixture may be called for – beware, some are not effective, in which case the coat will be dry and the skin tight.

7 **Weight loss,** dry coat and tight skin are all signs of dietary problems but might also be caused by worms or viruses; correct diagnosis is vital.

8 **Tying up** is often an expression of mineral imbalance and the cause needs to be identified, as constant supplementation often proves disappointing, that is, providing added calcium might be less effective than aiding absorption by eliminating worms and clearing out physical dirt, thereby promoting bowel health.

9 **Calcium/phosphorus imbalances** may also occur through the feeding of bran; they are detected by blood tests, when supplements may be prescribed to correct them.

10 **Keep supplementation** as simple as possible and do not mix supplements except with professional advice.

5 | Contaminants

There is plenty of evidence that fertilisers, herbicides and pesticides leach from land and gain access to water supplies. Heavy metals in the soil are dissolved by acid rain, and thus gain their entry to this cycle of contaminants; other substances may come on the rain or be carried on the wind – there is an endless list of possible toxic materials.

Recent research in Norway into sexual abnormalities in polar bears revealed high levels of PCBs (polychlorinated biphenyl) in their fat. The source of this was considered to be from material used to clean nuclear submarines, but PCBs have been used widely as industrial chemicals, from which source they have also entered water supplies. PCBs have the capacity to act in the same way as some natural hormones, and when they gain access to either human or animal bodies, intrude on normal mechanisms and affect sexual development. This trend had previously been noticed in fish, birds and reptiles, and it is also being linked to an apparent lowering of human sperm counts. These findings have led to a much welcomed investigation by the Environmental Protection Agency in Washington that will assess the dimensions of the overall problem.

Similarly, TBT (tributyltin), used as a ship anti-fouling paint, is found to be poisoning dolphins, whales and sea lions, and other marine life such as sea otters, birds and fish. Of course, this same fish could be used in fishmeal, or fish oils (cod liver oil), thus bringing the toxins back to the horse. It is just one of many paths for the transfer of toxins up and down the biological chain.

Marine pollution: a dead bull seal on the shore of the North Sea and a bird covered in oil from a tanker disaster

Spraying crops in California from the air

Professor Walters, in his *Reviews on Environmental Health*, 1985, suggested the average US citizen carries traces of five pesticides in his/her blood, showing how widespread these substances are. It is estimated that between 80 and 100 per cent of arable fields in southern England are regularly coated in up to thirty-six herbicides, fungicides and insecticides. Now, these substances are being aligned to declining bird populations, the suggestion being that caterpillars, grubs and insects are being lost, and that these are vital food sources for birds (as well as the part they play in the living soil). All of this is disconcerting from a human viewpoint, but, here, the question needs asking as to whether or not the same toxins are gaining access to the horse, and what effect they might be having on hormone levels and reproduction, and also, development, disease and performance levels. It would be too simplistic to hope that the answer is 'none'. But what are the immediate effects? And what will the long-term outcome be?

Nicolas Lampkin in his book *Organic Farming* says: 'The state of the environment is such that pesticide residues in the soil, air pollution from spray drift and industrial sources and heavy metals from sewage sludge etc will inevitably contaminate crops to some extent, even if the production methods used do not involve pesticides or contaminated manures.' The truth of this makes it clear how difficult it is to attain organic standards.

THE BODY'S DEFENCES AGAINST TOXINS

The healthy body has a range of protective mechanisms for dealing with foreign substances, though how it does so depends to a great extent on the nature of the substance, and in particular if it is soluble or not. Soluble substances that are tissue-destructive, such as acids, once they gain entry, will destroy the cells they come in contact with, and the extent of the damage will depend on their quantity, and how far they gain access to body organs. If the substance is seriously corrosive, it will destroy the linings of the mouth and may even cause death from shock. If it is less corrosive and reaches the small intestine before acting on tissues, it may result in local inflammation and ulcers. The clinical effect of this will vary with the degree and size of the damaged area.

If, on the other hand, a chemical is not tissue-irritant and becomes absorbed from the intestine, it may prove toxic to the liver (such as the alkaloid poison found in ragwort). The other possibility is that a chemical may interact with natural body substances and so disturb normal physiology (as with PCBs).

As far as ingested solid toxins are concerned, these are firstly met by scavenger cells that swallow and destroy them. If they manage to cross the gut lining and gain access to the circulation, they end up in the liver.

THE LIVER

The liver is the largest gland in the body, and it plays a complex role that includes both normal metabolism and the detoxification of harmful substances. It stores and releases carbohydrate, builds the plasma proteins, and is central to the metabolism of fat. All foreign material from the gut is received for detoxification, including toxins that come in food and water.

While there is no disputing the fact that toxins from manufacturing and from agriculture have been found in both humans and animals, there is scant research material showing their influence or establishing the common-held belief that they damage the immune system. One exception was work carried out on rats, using tributyltin (TBT), which established a lowered ability to resist bacterial and parasitic infections. In fact the lack of work in this field does not disprove the belief, it simply suspends argument, and it is important that potentially toxic material is treated as such until proven otherwise. There being no recorded research into their influence in the horse, the only question we can ask is: do these

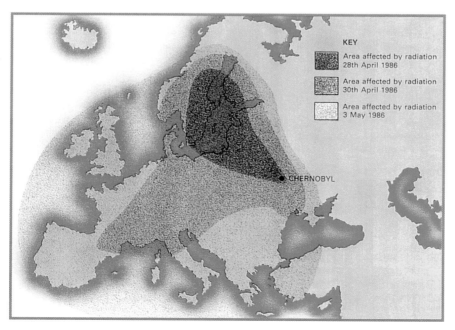

KEY

Area affected by radiation 28th April 1986

Area affected by radiation 30th April 1986

Area affected by radiation 3 May 1986

CHERNOBYL

Fall out from Chernobyl. The radioactive cloud spread over Europe

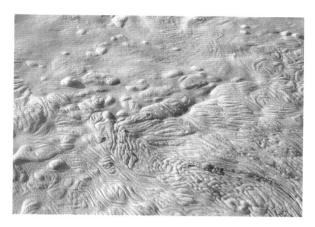

An example of heavy pollution from chemical and soapworks, River Mersey, UK. Contaminated water supplies can be extremely harmful for horses

substances, even in the tiniest amounts, hold significance for growth, development and performance standards in the horse? And do they make infection more likely, and does it take longer for the horse to shake them off? It is a subject that cannot be escaped as infection increases, even accepting that this is only one of the many possible factors involved.

The extent to which the liver is affected by toxin accumulation is, again, variable. For example, just a small amount of a substance such as arsenic has a stimulant effect; the latter was used for years as a stimulant tonic for horses. However, it is toxic and damages the liver, and beyond the period of stimulation is a time of gradual poisoning, leading to possible death.

INFECTION PARALLELS

Work on human athletes in Canada has shown a lowering of immunity after exhaustive endurance exercise. This is significant, because although it would be wrong to draw direct conclusions, the intensively trained horse suffers many infection problems similar to the human athlete, and it is only by controlled research that precise knowledge will be found. But the same toxins are available to both species of athlete and might easily underly such happenings.

Camargue mares and foals living 'organically'

Clearly, in our aim to produce an organic horse, there can be no tolerance of toxic materials. And while we will want this horse to withstand hard training, it will need to be able to do so in the long term, without frequent breakdowns caused by lameness or infection resulting from digestive sources.

TROUBLE-MAKERS

A list of possible toxic substances, diseases (and some drugs passed into the environment) follows, in alphabetic order. It is not intended to be exhaustive, simply a guide to an area that is deep and concerning:

Additive	Mostly synthetic chemicals added to food; varying from anti-oxidants to colourants, stabilisers to preservatives; it also includes synthetic vitamins.
Aflatoxin	Lethal fungal toxin commonly traced to contaminated grain or groundnut; symptoms include bleeding from nostrils and rectum, nervous signs.
Alar	The brand name of the chemical pesticide daminozide, used to spray apples and a suspected cause of cancer in animals and man; prescribed today.
Aldrin	Chlorinated hydrocarbon insecticide; prescribed.
Alphachloralose	A compound with anaesthetic properties used as a narcotic in animal baits; it is also used to poison birds.
Aluminium	A metal extracted from bauxite ore, compounds of which are used as pesticides, most commonly against slugs and mice, but also added to drinking water at times as a purifier; it leaches out of soils into streams and rivers as a side-effect of acid rain and is very toxic to fish and birds; long-term low-level exposure has been linked to Alzheimer's disease in humans; high concentrations are potentially lethal, causing local tissue destruction and nervous system changes.
Antibiotic	A chemical substance used to eliminate (usually undesirable) bacteria.
Anti-oxidants	Chemicals added to food to delay decay in oils and fats (E300–321). Excessive amounts are a known health risk; some are suspected of being unsafe; vitamins C and E are anti-oxidants essential in body defences against infections and toxins, also in recovery from illness.
Arsenic	A highly poisonous substance used in weedkillers and fruit-tree sprays; also occurs in industrial waste. Symptoms include abdominal pain, paralysis and blindness; skin conditions are a sign of low-grade poisoning.
Atrazine	A triazine herbicide capable of being toxic; prescribed.
Avermectins	A group of chemically related anthelminthics that include the successful wormer ivermectin; it is said to kill dung beetles.
Azinophos-methyl	Organophosphorus insecticide and acaricide; toxic; prescribed.
Benzene	A cancer-causing substance in motor fuel.
Benzene hexachloride	A chlorinated hydrocarbon used as an insecticide.
Benzimidazole	A group of related compounds used against helminth parasites; recently some types have been found resistant against particular worms.
Botulism	A highly fatal poisoning caused by ingestion of bacterial toxins.
Butadiene	A cancer-causing substance in motor fuel.
Cadmium	A heavy metal that is very toxic to humans, causing kidney and heart damage and calcium depletion, leading to brittle bones. It has entered marine food chains because of dumping at sea; it is also used in pesticides now banned in Western Europe; it occurs naturally in phosphate fertilisers from which it is released during refinement; prescribed.
Carbamates	Pesticides based on organic nitrogen compounds capable of causing poisoning, eg muscle tremor, salivation, ataxia and dyspnoea. Includes insecticides such as carbaryl, aldicarb; herbicides such as barban, asulan, diallite, triallate; fungicides such as maneb and zineb; and soil fumigants such as metham-sodium; they are usually irritant topically. Aldicarb and zineb are possible carcinogens; they have the capacity to kill non-intended species, but do not generally persist in the environment. Asulan is used extensively against bracken; carbaryl against head lice.
Carbofuran	A carbamate, widely used for soil treatment in crop farming; it destroys ticks and mites, and is a wormer toxic to birds.

Chlorinated hydrocarbons	Because of their slow water solubility, they are used extensively as pesticides that need to persist on their designated area of use; effective in use, but their resistance is known, and affects non-target species; some have entered the food chain and are toxic to man and animals. They are widely used as solvents and in other industrial areas, and solvents are known to damage the liver, heart and kidneys, and may also cause cancers; they produce dioxins when burnt, especially PCBs. They have been phased out in developed countries, but are still used in poorer regions. Known by the names aldrin, benzene hexachloride, chlordane, DDD, DDT, endosulfan, heptachlor, isodrin, gammexane, lindane, methoxychlor.
Chlorinated naphthalenes	Added to lubricants, fire-retardants, insulants; they are poisonous and a cause of vitamin A deficiency if taken in low doses over time.
Chlorine	Used as a purifying agent in water; toxic in anything other than dilute amounts. A 1977 survey found that people in New York counties drinking chlorinated water suffered a 44 per cent higher death rate from gastro-intestinal and urinary tract cancers.
Coal-tar dyes	Used as food colourants; some are thought to cause animal cancers. They are capable of causing allergic-type reactions.
Colitis X	An acute diarrhoeic condition of horses, possibly of bacterial origin.
DDD	(dichlorodiphenyldichloroethane) Chlorinated hydrocarbon insecticide, first used in North American farming in the 1930s; it is now recognised as a dangerous pollutant and a possible carcinogen, poisonous to fish and birds; concentrates in fatty tissues; prescribed.
DDT	(dichlorodiphenyltrichloroethane) Chlorinated hydrocarbon insecticide, as above; prescribed.
Dichlorphenthion	Used in sheep-dip; a human toxin.
Dichlorvos	Organophosphate pesticide also known as DDVP, suspected of being carcinogenic; prescribed.
Dieldrin	Chlorinated hydrocarbon used in garden sprays, as a wood preservative, or moth killer. The suspected cause of human cancers, and has been banned from use in Western countries since the 1970s; it is still used in wood preservatives. It contaminates otters, herons and eels (all with high fat content), and is especially dangerous as a source of contamination for man; prescribed.
Dioxin	Industrially produced toxin capable of causing cancers and long-lasting skin conditions in animals and humans. TCDD (tetrachlorodibenzoparadioxin) is a contaminant of hormone weedkiller 2/4/5-T *; dioxin is produced in the burning of organochlorine-containing waste, also plastics; and in car emissions causing air pollution, and so is deposited on plants and soil, and enters water supplies.
Endosulfan	Chlorinated hydrocarbon insecticide; prescribed.
Endrin	Chlorinated hydrocarbon insecticide; highly toxic; prescribed.
Epicauta	The blister beetle, found in alfalfa hay; it produces an irritant poison if trapped or crushed in hay-making, and the hay may remain toxic for years. The minimum lethal dose is less than 1mg/kg hay; symptoms vary from anorexia and depression, to shock and death.
Ergot	A fungal toxin on rye and other grasses; it is also known to affect humans. Symptoms vary from gangrene of the extremities, to manifestations of damage to the central nervous system.
External parasites	Lice, ticks, mites, maggots.
Fenitrothion	Organophosphate insecticide with low toxicity for animals; prescribed.
Fertiliser	Material to improve soil fertility by adding to its chemical composition, such as nitrate and superphosphate, but blood, bone, kelp, humus and excrement (both human and animal) are also used. Calcium cyanamide, ammonium sulphate and urea are all capable of causing poisoning; nitrate is normally provided in the form of ammonium nitrate; phosphate is derived from naturally occurring rock phosphate; potassium comes from mined potash deposits. Heavy doses of water-soluble nitrates and phosphates easily reach groundwater supplies.
Fluoride	(generic name for salts of the gas fluorine) Element added to water as a means to fighting tooth decay; suspected of causing mottled teeth, injury to the brain and nervous system, bone deformity, arthritis, allergies, duodenal ulcers, cancer and diabetes; also associated with goitre, personality disorders and kidney failure. Initially it was added as sodium fluoride (a rat poison). A

medical survey (1985) concluded that fluoride damages enzyme systems and DNA; also mouth ulcers, stomach and bowel disorders, cramps and diarrhoea have all been associated with fluoridated toothpaste.

Formaldehyde	Used as a soil sterilising agent; it is also found in motor fuel. It is capable of causing cancers, also contact dermatitis.
Fungicide	A substance used to destroy fungi; used on crops against diseases such as mildew and rust. Mostly metal based, and may include mercury or sulphur; many are carcinogenic.
Gamma hexachloro-cyclohexane	Active ingredient of gammexane or lindane; prescribed.
Gaucho	Insecticide causing mad bee disease, named because affected bees are incapable of finding their way back to their hives.
Glyphosate	Herbicide used on grains; blamed for soft shells in bird eggs.
Grass-seed nematode	Worm that infests Wimmera ryegrass (productive annual pasture grass). It causes fatal poisoning, the worm in company with bacteria leading to ataxia, convulsions and death.
Grass sickness	Disease of unknown cause, possibly due to ingested toxin; it damages part of the nervous system, leading to gradual paralysis of the intestine.
Herbicide	Chemical compound that destroys weeds, either selective, killing particular species, or general; it is also divided into contact herbicides (that affect only what they touch) and systemics (that enter the plant itself); contact herbicides include sulphuric acid, the carbamate group and dinitro products (such as DNOC and dinoseb), which can be very poisonous to animals; hormone weedkillers are systemic in action and suspected of causing human pathology. Most herbicides are essentially of low toxicity to animals, though recently sprayed pasture might easily be toxic; exceptions include dinitro products and organic paraquat. Fish and insects are less resistant. Poisoning is often due to accidental access to concentrated weedkiller. The best known herbicide groups are bipyridyls, chlorinated acids, dinitro compounds, phenoxyacid derivatives, thiocarbamates and triazines.
Hexachlorobenzene	Fungicide used on stored grain. It is a known contaminant of foods of animal origin, and a cause of liver damage; prescribed.
Hexachlorophane	Once used for tapeworms and fluke; toxic signs include tremor, diarrhoea, recumbency.
Hydrocarbons	Mostly atmospheric pollution from vehicle emission; highly toxic and cancer-inducing.
Imidazothiazoles	Group of anthelminthics including levamisole.
Insecticides	Arsenic, nicotine and derris are used to kill insects; organochlorines and organophosphates appeared later. Organochlorines are poisonous to other than their target species – for instance DDT concentrates in the food chain, causing problems for birds of prey and aquatic mammals; some resistance. Organophosphates such as dichlorvos, parathion and carbamates are irritant and potentially toxic.
Internal parasites	Roundworms, fluke, bots.
Iodine	Poisoning causes skin scaling, nasal and ocular discharges.
Ivermectin	From avermectin grouping.
Laminitis	Complex disease of horses marked by changes and pain in the feet.
Lead	Metallic element of high toxicity; commonly an air pollutant from vehicle emissions (90 per cent from cars) – it may travel a mile from, say, a motorway before falling. It contaminates the leaves of vegetables and fruit; it is the base of some paints, which may be licked by animals; it is dissolved from water pipes by acid water.
Lindane	Chlorinated hydrocarbon; causes aplastic anaemia, leukaemia and convulsions in animals; also thought to be linked to human breast cancer. Chemically it is similar to oestrogens. It is very persistent in nature. Efforts are being made to prescribe.
Linuron	Herbicide which may increase the nitrate content of sprayed plants.
Malathion	Organophosphorus insecticide of low toxicity for animals; prescribed.
MCPA	Weedkiller considered of low toxicity, but toxic in large doses to cattle.

Mercury	Liquid metallic element that is highly toxic if inhaled, swallowed or absorbed through the skin. It is included in some insecticides used on grain, whence it may accumulate in animal fats; it is used extensively as an industrial metal in chemical and plastic industries, whence it may gain entry to rivers, lakes and oceans from factory effluent, causing poisoning of fish and humans; also used as a seed dressing for the prevention of moulds, whence it may cause poisoning of animals and man. Symptoms in horses include loss of hair, gastroenteritis and emaciation; prescribed.
Molluscicides	Chemicals used to kill snails; copper sulphate was used but is toxic, and has now been replaced by more selective chemicals.
Nitrates	Main source of nitrogen, through which plants form protein; they occur naturally, and can also be added to soil through fertilisers. Being soluble in water, they are prone to leaching into rivers and groundwater, especially after rain; they are capable of causing damage to rivers and lakes. A suspected contributor to 'blue baby syndrome'; said to cause fetal malformations and birth defects, as well as gastric cancers in adults; also headaches, nausea and fatigue. Combined with pesticides in water they may form nitrosamines, which are both carcinogenic and cause birth defects.
Nitrogen	An odourless, colourless gas forming 78 per cent of the earth's atmosphere; essential to the formation of protein, therefore life. Part of the polluting substances that give rise to acid rain (such as nitrous oxide).
NSAID	Non-steroidal anti-inflammatory drug (such as butazolidin); capable of causing gastric disorders on prolonged use.
Nutraceutical medicine	Disease therapy through the use of dietary elements.
Organochlorines	Also known as chlorinated hydrocarbons.
Organophosphates	(OPs) First used in the 1940s, powerful pesticides inhibiting the nervous system of organisms; found toxic to vertebrates. They have been inhaled, swallowed or absorbed from the skin; a human poison. Used as anthelminthics; also in hydraulic fluids, coolants and lubricants, from which animals may become exposed. All are potentially poisonous. Dichlorvos (DDVP), demetron-S-methyl, disulfoton, fenitrothion, glyphosphate, malathion and parathion are all OPs; mostly used to control flies, mites, aphids, ticks, though there is resistance in some cases; glyphosphate is mainly a herbicide, and considered safe (see above).
Paraquat	Widely used herbicide poisonous to man; considered safe when used to kill weeds.
Parasiticides	Substances or agents used to destroy parasites.
Pesticides	Substances used to destroy pests; these include insecticides, herbicides, fungicides, molluscicides, acaricides (kill ticks and mites), nematocides (kill roundworms) and rodenticides; also arsenicals, carbamates, hydrocarbons, organochlorines, OPs, and pyrethroids. Many, like DDT, have been withdrawn because of toxicity and resistance; atrazine and simazine are the most common pesticides found in water.
PBB	(polybrominated biphenyl) Used as flame retardants, electrical insulators, heat transfer agents. They accumulate in fat, and are responsible for diarrhoea, weight loss and abortion.
PCB	(polychlorinated biphenyl) Organochlorine compounds used widely as industrial chemicals since the 1930s; originally thought safe, they are now banned. They accumulate in fat, and have a slow rate of excretion and breakdown; they are toxic to humans and animals, causing liver damage and symptoms that would indicate damage to the central nervous system. They produce dioxins on burning. Have found their way into rivers and seas: seals, Polar bears, cetaceans and other marine mammals in their native regions have all been found to have high levels in fat; also found in Arctic seals and Antarctic penguins, in Pacific whales and fish at depths of 3,000m. Suspected of leading to widespread infertility: possible cause of hermaprhroditism in bears; experimental poisoning led to diarrhoea, poor weight gain, abortion; said to have caused 80 per cent sterility in North Sea seals, also reduced disease resistance, thus allowing a distemper-like virus to cause serious losses in the late eighties; prescribed.
PCNB	(pentachloronitrobenzene) Soil fungicide used on crops; not associated with any recognised disease. It is known to enter the human food chain and to leave residues in all species.

Pentachlorophenol	Wood preservative, constituent of waste oil; it may be present on shavings or sawdust. A known toxin responsible for weight loss, incoordination and skin reactions; prescribed.
Permethrin	Synthetic pyrethroid used as an insecticide, for example against woodworm. Concentrates in house dust, and remains for two years after application on tables and worktops; transferred through house dust to food eaten by humans, to whom it may be toxic.
Phalaris	Type of grass that may cause a form of staggers.
Phenothiazine	Outdated wormer; capable of causing abortion in mares; also photosensitisation in dosed horses.
Phosphates	Supplied naturally to water and soil by the weathering of rocks; artificially available through fertilisers of rock phosphate origin, which are water-soluble. Can damage rivers, though fairly stable in soil, and do not leach readily.
Phthalates	Derived from phthalic acid, used to soften PVC. Capable of causing toxicity in children. Symptoms to include kidney and liver damage, infertility and cancer.
Piperazine	Outdated wormer used to kill roundworms; safe in large doses. Although poisoning has occurred, the affected horses have generally recovered.
Protim	Wood preservative containing pentachlorophenol, TBTO and dieldrin.
Pyrethrins	Active ingredient of pyrethrum plant (member of Chrysanthemum family), used as insecticide; capable of causing systemic or cutaneous allergic reactions. Synthetic pyrethrins are called pyrethroids, for example cypermethrin, cyhalothrin, deltamethrin, flumethrin, permethrin.
Radioactive fallout	Material similar to that released after explosion in nuclear reactor at Chernobyl 1986, or fire at Windscale 1957; radioactive isotopes are toxic and carcinogenic.
Radionuclides	Come from the disposal of radioactive waste, or disasters of the nature of Chernobyl and Windscale.
Ragwort	Common pasture weed that causes severe liver damage.
Rhodococcus equi	Organism associated with pneumonia, diarrhoea, sometimes marked by chronic localised abscesses in foals.
Rotavirus	Viral cause of highly infectious diarrhoea of young foals.
Ryegrass staggers	Occurs in horses on pasture containing perennial ryegrass, causing incoordination; probably caused by fungal toxin.
Salmonella	Bacterial organism, cause of sometimes acute infections of foals.
Selenium	Toxicity most likely to occur from high feeding levels; signs include skin lesions, hoof growth defects, lethargy.
Simazine	Triazine herbicide capable of causing toxicity; prescribed.
St John's wort	Plant causing photosensitisation, often leading to sloughing of white skin areas of horses.
Strangles	Highly contagious bacterial disease of horses, marked by purulent abscesses and copious nasal discharges.
Sulphur	Occurs naturally in some rocks, but is also deposited from erupting volcanoes. Sulphates are highly pollutant: sulphuric acid is an element of acid rain; most atmospheric sulphur comes from the burning of oil and coal.
Tributyltin	(TBT, an organotin) Fungicide and molluscicide known to be highly toxic for non-target wildlife such as whales, dolphins and sealions. It is gradually being withdrawn, though it is still recognised as a cause of poisoning; prescribed.
Trifluralin	Toxic weedkiller; causes diarrhoea, nervous signs; prescribed.
Triphenyltin	Organotin, prescribed.
Tetrahydropyrimidines	Group of anthelminthics including pyrantel, a horse wormer.
Triazines	Selective herbicides including atrazine, simazine, prometone, prometryne; toxic signs including weight loss, anorexia and weakness.

WHAT YOU CAN DO AVOIDING CONTAMINANTS

1 **It is accepted** that the overall control of contaminants is in the hands of governments and their efforts have to be moved by public opinion.

2 **As for the individual,** there is a distinction between those with their own land who can produce their own raw materials and those dependent on bought in, often compounded, feeds.

3 **By growing** organic grains and providing grasses free of artificial fertilisers (organically manured) the level of contamination may be significantly reduced.

4 **Those who have to buy** all their food materials can create a demand for organic production (largely unavailable at present).

5 **Be critical** about what you buy; be clear about the standards of purity you want, and look for wholesome raw materials produced as cleanly as possible.

6 **Remember** that hay, silage and concentrates may all be sources of specific diseases where they carry ergot, blister beetles or infectious contaminants – leptospirosis, a bacterial infection affecting the liver, may be contracted from food soiled with rat urine.

7 **Apply the standards** of water purity recommended in Chapter 8.

8 **Bring horses indoors** when there is a danger of spray drift.

9 **Be aware** that the influences of toxins may reduce disease resistance, affect growth and limit performance.

10 **The effects** of low-grade poisoning, perhaps from contact with sprays or containers, can be slow lingering sickness that may take months to recover from if the liver has been damaged.

11 **The effects** of water-borne toxins in competing animals may only be seen as they reach full fitness and under extreme demands.

6 Infection and its Prevention

In organic teaching, no attempt is made to deny that infectious diseases arise. However, there is a realistic understanding that they increase as management systems intensify. There is, then, reason to identify what causes this in order to prevent it. There is also full recognition that sick animals need treatment. But the long-term aim is prevention by avoiding the basic causes, such as overcrowding, imperfect housing and bad feeding practices. For the horse, intensive training might have the same disease implications as it has for the human athlete – as we have seen, scientific work having been able to define chemical changes that occur within the body, opening the way to infection. This, as suggested, is associated with endurance training, although disease patterns in horses indicate that the problem is not confined just to endurance animals.

FACTORS AFFECTING RESISTANCE

- Virulence of the organism and existing immunity.
- Feeding.
- Stabling.
- Transport.
- Training regimes.
- Food and water contaminants.

A US research project showed that horses in the field were less likely to be infected than those in unsuitable stabling, but the least likely to be infected were those kept in better quality stables of, for example, veterinary hospitals. This agrees with work in the human field showing that chilling has an adverse effect on the normal working of respiratory defensive mechanisms. Horses are protected from the extremes of outdoor weather by being stabled. But chilling, it would appear, is most common indoors in draughty conditions.

The possible causes of infection are twofold: either from very virulent organisms to which there is no resistance or immunity; or through lowered resistance, allowing invasion by opportunist organisms.

TRANSPORT

The effects of transport on infection have long been recognised, as have the evident stresses involved. Commercial lorries, if not hygienically maintained, are a possible means of transferring infection, but horses discomforted and sweating in transit (by land, sea or air) are thought to suffer an increased risk of infection, as well as disturbances to gut organisms and all that might ensue from that. The importance of this is in the prospect for spreading infection at the destination; but also, in the regeneration of conditions such as EHV-1 (see pp78-82), that can lie latent in the tissues and recur at times of stress.

(top)
Swimming may be harmful to horses with particular types of injuries;
(above) Horses in enclosed areas may easily spread infection to each other, especially when stressed by travel

TRAINING REGIMES

From an historical viewpoint, the change in use that man has imposed upon the horse, from a labouring animal to an athletic performer, has been an important development in its health patterns. This is because of the special stresses of intensive training as well as the managemental pressures that go with it (such as heavier feeding to promote performance). Furthermore the introduction of interval training to human athletics has resulted in similar work regimes being applied to the horse: the increase in weight-lifting and other strength exercises has been duplicated by making gallops and other working grounds more testing, and by using treadmills and swimming pools as additional disciplines.

The modern racehorse doesn't just have a leisurely breeze up the perfectly manicured grass, he repeats the exercise according to the dictates of his trainer, the idea being to attain a higher level of fitness. The incline, if not the length, of the gallop is likely to be a lot stiffer than of old, and the pace and number of intervals may vary from the enjoyable to the seriously testing. The surfaces, bends and undulations are all added factors that may have an influence in inducing either injury or fatigue.

An increasing use of treadmills, even water-submerged types, is often a beneficial extra loading, especially during the early conditioning stages of a fitness regime. But the stiffer the exercise the closer the animal comes to breaking point, when the most obvious outcome is injury. It is also important to recognise that any athletic animal needs warming up before being subjected to hard work, so the loading must be gradual and the initial pace not so sharp that it might do harm.

Swimming pools are useful for developing the fitness changes in the respiratory system. However, swimming is not a fully natural exercise for horses, although they swim well. Moreover, as it is not a weight-bearing exercise, the muscles used are not those used in ridden paces; it is also potentially dangerous for horses with soft tissue upper limb and back injuries. There is then the more obvious danger that infection will supervene when wet horses are not dried quickly. When carried to excess, it is a possible way of over-stressing the body, resulting in fatigue and its consequences. It also needs to be said that many horses do not appear to enjoy swimming and have a look of apprehension all the time they are in the water. Some of this, undoubtedly, is as a result of pain, most likely due to unidentified soft tissue injuries. Far more attention needs to be paid to this, as some injured horses should not be swimming and are in danger of drowning simply because the effort is beyond them.

MANAGEMENT PRESSURES

As already mentioned, feeding regimes are constantly changing to explore the extent to which performance can be improved. Changes in stabling are motivated by economics and for the convenience of those who work in them. The link between these changes and disease incidence is always likely to be significant, though we never seem to look at disease as a first priority.

ADVANCES IN DISEASE CONTROL

The development of antibiotics has meant that conditions which earlier would have led to probable death are now successfully treated. The creation of the electron microscope meant, for the first time, the recognition and identification of viruses. But it has to be appreciated that the relatively good control of bacterial infections has been superseded by less-easy-to-control viruses (and bacteria), and a change of disease expression that might well be linked to the changes in training and management. The question arises: is this because tissues are inflamed by factors under human control, giving the organisms the chance to grow? Or is it simply the menace of organisms gaining greater capacity to cause disease? There is every reason to believe it is the former.

While we can understand that very mild infections would have little effect on inactive horses (such as broodmares), their significance is altogether different for those in full training. There is even a difference between what the eventer can cope with as opposed to the racehorse. The reason is in pace, and the need for maximal effort – and this means the need for a fully clean and healthy pair of lungs. Thus a mild virus may mean little in casual riding animals or work horses, but low-grade infections are the plague of racehorses, especially those kept in large numbers, and where many yards close together provide a ready population for immediate spread. The problem increases when this is combined with winter weather conditions.

CEM

With the decline of lethal bacterial infections, the modern accent on such diseases is epitomised by conditions such as contagious equine metritis (CEM). This is a bacterial (and highly transmissible) venereal disease that was first recognised in the seventies and is notifiable in the UK, Ireland, the USA and Australia. The organism is susceptible to antibiotics and has been kept fairly well under control by rigorous supervision, legal controls and a Common Code of Practice that applies in France, Germany, Ireland, Italy and the UK. There are statutory controls in the USA and Australia covering both imports and CEM outbreaks within each country. New Zealand has not seen the condition and has not made it notifiable, but exercises standard rigorous import controls. The disease, being easily spread by covering, proved a major problem where it became established in commercial studs. It causes infertility and is marked by copious vaginal discharges. While it is treatable, it has a highly disruptive influence on breeding and is capable of being transmitted widely by recovered mares and stallions that still harbour the causal organism.

THE CONTROL OF INFECTION

A major influence in the spread, and control, of infection is the diverse nature of the horse world we now know. There are all sorts of activities and sports that bring horses together from a wide variety of regions and countries, and the potential for contact, from a disease viewpoint, is universal. Only the sensible controls of international authorities keeps this potential in check.

The Thoroughbred horse is the most important breed economically, and is highly controlled and regulated. The Thoroughbred breeder, being accountable to registering authorities as well as to the dictates of the major studs, is generally obliged to observe established codes of practice – there is little to be gained from ignoring or flaunting the public interest. But outside this limited area, the need for disease control is less commonly recognised.

A farmer with a few non-Thoroughbred mares might not worry about vaccination or other routines, such as swabbing and blood tests, and low value horses on moors and commons do not warrant such expense. Also, non-competing leisure riders have no obligation to worry about disease and its spread. As a result, there exists a potential pool of infection, never within supervision, from which disease can regularly seep out to the wider world. Between these two extremes there is a half-way state, where competing animals generally are subject to some degree of control (mainly flu vaccination and export regulations), although they do not have the same vested need for control that the Thoroughbred industry has.

Racing is universally bothered by this situation, and is hampered in trying to eliminate it by the dimensions of the uncontrolled sector. It is also affected by the generation and spread of infection within its own limits, despite some regulation.

EVA

Breeding is inhibited further by conditions such as equine viral arteritis (EVA) and herpesvirus infections. EVA is marked by nasal discharge, localised oedema, inflamed membranes and possible abortion. First recognised in 1953, it is virtually world wide in

---

FACTORS ALLOWING INFECTION TO DEVELOP

- Intensivism.
- Poor management.
- Failure to recognise and clear up early infection.
- Ideas that spread is inevitable and efforts to control are wasteful.
- Bad hygiene.
- Widespread movement of horses.

distribution. It is spread through nasal discharges and by the stallion during mating. Some stallions remain carriers after recovery and continue to spread virus through the semen: obviously detection of these is vital in any control programme. The disease is covered by a Common Code of Practice in the UK, Ireland, France, Germany and Italy.

EHV

Herpesvirus infection, especially EHV-1, is a disease that thrives in conditions that might be termed intensive. It, too, is covered (for the UK and Ireland) by a Code of Practice. It occurs mainly as a respiratory condition and is most commonly spread by airborne droplet when affected horses cough or clear their noses (the virus can be carried several miles on the wind). Aborted foetuses are also fertile sources of infection, and their contamination of stables and pastures is well known. In particularly bad outbreaks, abortion rates may be very high and can occur in early pregnancy. This is an evident and serious concern.

However, the most worrying modern expression of this disease is its capacity to cause paralysis, which may prove fatal. This is fairly common, having first occurred in the USA during the late sixties and then crossed to Europe shortly after. The virus is known to exist in a latent state in recovered horses, and these can become clinical again when their resistance is lowered. This might happen because of poor nutrition, while recovering from other infections, and through poor management practices.

The disease is also seen outside breeding, in training and commercial yards. While in these circumstances there is no worry of abortion, the respiratory and systemic influences are serious for competing animals, and the danger of paralysis still exists. Vaccination has been tried for a number of years, but there is no solid base of evidence as to its efficacy. While there are those who say it reduces abortions, and others find it useful against respiratory infection, there have been disappointments and the situation appears to have room for improvement.

When mares go to stud, they usually meet others from a variety of sources, and it is possible that they bring different species and strains of organisms with them. Then, by being in close contact, the chance exists that they may set up a series of infections, thus paving the way for increasingly serious clinical happenings.

It is recognised that close contact is critical in deciding the seriousness of an outbreak. By spreading horses over a wider area, and by dispersing those kept indoors, there is a dilution of infection and a reduction of serious disease. But the picture is clouded by the capacity of organisms previously considered harmless to enter the clinical picture

HOW INFECTION SPREADS WITHIN A YARD

■ Through coughing and discharges.
■ On the hands and clothes of handlers.
■ On implements and tack.

HOW INFECTION COMES FROM OUTSIDE

■ Mares convening from different sources.
■ Horses at competitions, shows and race-meetings.
■ Viruses are carried long distances on the wind.
■ Bacteria may be passed between horses meeting on working grounds.
■ Vehicles may transmit infection.
■ Horses passing on the road may infect others in fields.

and become significant in already debilitated animals – there is a wide variety that can act on the respiratory system, in particular. When resistance is lowered, and tissues are inflamed from previous infection, the potential for new invaders is high and serial infections can happen.

The intensive nature of breeding has also led to an increased importance for diseases such as rotavirus, a cause of diarrhoea in foals, and *Rhodococcus*, whose importance has come, perhaps, more on account of lowered resistance than enhanced virulence. It is a situation that may continue to get worse.

ORGANIC CONSIDERATIONS

It is evident from the above that the potential for infection is great when horses are brought together in large numbers and then pushed for commercial purposes, be that expressed as either reproduction or performance. Horse breeding is mainly an economic exercise, and equine sport is essentially a dream pursuit that finds its limitations in the depth of its owners' pockets. Management is, ultimately, dictated by cost, and the element of profit is somewhat elastic.

While it is clear now that horses kept in small numbers, and isolated from others, suffer less infection, the exact point at which this situation changes is not known. We accept that horses don't like draughts, but there is no universal understanding of precisely what that means. We do not have data relating to the ideal numbers of horses kept in a building, the space each should have, the types of division, ventilation and lighting. For the answers, we rely on anecdotal evidence and fashion. We also introduce new feeding regimes without fully considering the implications. What if we disturb muscle metabolism? Liver function? Disease resistance?

The organic horse must not only have developed to its full capacity through the growing years, it must have the nutritional inputs to continue the natural process. Its relationship with its environment must not favour disease. The healthy animal must hold the advantage over infection, and we must cater for the weak points, such as when dehydration might follow exercise, or transport, or mineral deficiency might ensue from something as simple as polluted water.

There are now world competitions in almost every discipline of equine sport. This, naturally, convenes animals from all corners of the globe, and is an open pathway to infections that may easily elude the mostly effective standard supervision. It is a pathway that cannot be closed without seriously curtailing the progress of individual sports.

The risks of the future rest in the nature of organisms and in our failure to be prepared when something new comes. As we know, some slow viruses survive boiling and disinfection. Other organisms survive exposure; there is always the worm that over-winters, the bacterium that forms resistant spores, such as anthrax. Such dangers are ever present, and will avail themselves of opportunities to infect and spread as they are shown them: it is their existence. Our duty is to know this, and to prevent their ability to do it.

Case Note: Herpesvirus Paralysis

When the first European outbreak of *Herpesvirus paralysis* happened in Ireland in the early seventies, it had already been seen in the USA – although there was nothing on record to confirm it. To people unlucky enough to have seen this disease, it is devastating and shocking: the sight of horses floundering and going down is very upsetting and there is no way of knowing what percentage is likely to be affected. Initially there was no known line of treatment; no one knew if recumbent horses could be saved: no one could help make a diagnosis.

For the vets left to deal with it, and with hundreds of valuable animals exposed, the questions were endless. There were no guidelines to follow, and there was no rational treatment except to try to keep paralysed mares on their feet by standing them in makeshift slings. They were given intravenous fluid therapy, and everyone then hoped the condition would pass off.

The first outbreaks were in County Cork and near Dublin. The disease turned up in the UK some years later. On the European continent, the most highly publicised outbreak involved the famed White Horses of Vienna.

The question may be asked: what caused this organism suddenly to change its pathological effects? What were we doing to encourage such serious clinical outcomes? While we can accept that the virus mutated, did new elements of management increase disease risk and provide an opportunity for organisms like this? It was a time when Thoroughbred breeding was rapidly expanding. Studs were getting bigger and becoming more intensive; mares were coming from wider bases within Europe; trans-Atlantic horse movement was on the increase.

As one of the first to have faced the problem, and not long out of university, it was necessary to ask a multiplicity of questions never even considered in veterinary school. One morning in the spring of 1972, a client's mare was found off her legs in a field at a local stud farm. Her name was Tamasin and she was the dam of a good National Hunt horse, called Tamalin. To the owners, Commander and Mrs Merry, she was a valuable asset and they wanted her saved. When I got to her, she looked as healthy as a cricket, except she was unable to stand; she wanted to get up, and was eating all round her. There was a suggestion of mild jaundice in her membranes. I had no idea of the cause. The possible alternatives were: a mild toxin, a bacterial infection (like leptospirosis, the cause of Weil's disease in man), a nutritional disturbance. Authorities consulted did not believe there was any infectious cause of liver disease in the country other than leptospirosis. We had no mosquitoes to transmit the kinds of viral disease that cause encephalitis in some USA areas.

By midday the mare's condition hadn't changed, and it was evident she would never get to her feet of her own accord. Her appetite was not affected; she had no temperature; her tail was strong and mobile; there was normal sensation in her distal limbs; there was no heat in the feet. She might have been able to get up if lifted in slings, but there was no way of knowing then if she would survive with feeding and support or if her condition was terminal. However, on this second visit, it emerged there had already been problems on the stud. She was not the first mare to have gone down; there was a hint of one or two abortions; and a foal or two, it was said, had been lost.

Something in the region of one hundred new mares were then presented for examination. As a high percentage showed the same hint of mild

jaundice, it seemed the livers of all these animals were suffering some kind of common challenge.

That day saw the start of an invasion of experts who came to shed light on the situation. An equine pathologist from Dublin Veterinary College wanted post mortem material, so Commander and Mrs Merry, very bravely, gave permission for Tamasin to be put down. Numerous blood samples were taken from other mares, and early reports suggested a viral infection, which was confirmed the following day. Liver samples showed areas of damaged tissue, explaining the jaundice, and EHV-1 was identified as the cause.

Fifty days and nights of clinical time was spent dealing with the problem. The public announcement led to international repercussions: the horse world wanted to know what was going on. More experts came, and more samples were taken. In the end it was established that three different types of herpes virus were present, and to add to the confusion, a Swiss virologist later isolated an adenovirus – not proved to be a cause of clinical

The most highly publicised outbreak of EHV-1 with abortion and paralysis was in the Lippizzaners in Austria

disease in anything other than immune-compromised Arab foals up to that time.

The effect within the local community was one of fear that the problem would spread outwards. On a wider scale, panic-induced reactions, fanned, to some extent, by the press, led to an active interest from the Department of Agriculture, and a storm of gossip and innuendo that eventually turned an accusing finger at the unfortunate minnows who were trying to treat the crisis.

A condition of this type also creates fears that it might spread quickly, especially when its origins are not immediately apparent. Could it be carried on the wind? Could those in contact carry it on their hands, clothes, even vehicles? Where are the limits and what is the potential for further chaos? Comparisons arise with conditions such as foot-and-mouth disease of cattle. It is not slow and insidious, but an explosion that is happening as you watch.

As the episode evolved, a variety of symptoms were seen. There were, for example, blisters in the mouths of many animals, some coalescing to form large ulcers when they burst. The explanation was probably the adenovirus. On the udders of many mares, small pin-point haemorrhages were seen by stud staff: these started as tiny spots of fresh blood, mostly on those springing down to foal; the spots subsequently turned white as they dried and were invaded by surface organisms. No explanation for their presence was ever provided, although a single suspect titre to viral arteritis showed up in a blood sample sent to the USA; this, again, at a much later date, might have offered an explanation.

In the wider area of the county, where no abortions and no recumbencies were reported, at least two foals were born showing extreme jaundice and passing urine the colour of Guinness. Their dams also showed severe jaundice. Despite this, neither foal ever looked remotely sick: both grew and carried on as normal, and one went on to win eight races over jumps (the career of the other was not followed).

It has generally been considered that later outbreaks were due to the sole activity of the EHV-1 organism. This did not appear to be the case in Cork, however, where repeating, and increasingly serious symptoms were more likely to have been due to sequential infections with the different viruses present. Thus a stud groom reported that a stallion's penis turned yellow after showing illness one night; and workers in the outbreak suffered headaches, and showed some of the signs seen in the horses (such as the mouth ulcers). In the early stages of the outbreak, many of the mares aborted. An error of judgement was made in bringing all mares indoors, a move intended to increase supervision and reduce illness. But, while mares at grass showed signs of infection, they did so without the complications on the whole. Most returned to normal in time, and showed no residual signs of the problem.

Affected foals contracted pneumonia and some were lost, others were born with the infection and died within days. However, those more than a month old, and strong when infected, were as likely to survive as the mares; in fact, few were lost in the end. In subsequent outbreaks, recorded losses have frequently been greater.

What was most significant was that this outbreak was centred in a rapidly expanding stud complex where there was little experience of such kinds of disease. It was intensification, in so much as that means more animals, higher stocking rates, commercial priorities, that led to such devastation.

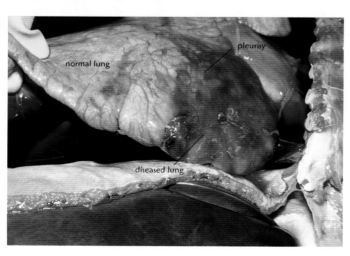

Area of pneumonitis and pleurisy in a lung. This from a case of EHV-4, also isolated in the outbreak discussed in the case study

WHAT YOU CAN DO

DEALING WITH INFECTION

1   **It is vital** to accept that infection is rife in intensive horse production, especially modern Thoroughbred racing and breeding.

2   **It may be impossible** to avoid contact with infections that are windborne, though whether or not your horses become infected depends largely on your own standards of management.

3   **Use vaccines** for conditions like 'flu, if your horse is likely to become exposed to possible infection.

4   **Remember** that there are vaccine breakdowns and some horses react adversely to specific vaccines, in which case the disease might be less of a threat than the vaccine.

5   **Respect** international control measures for infectious diseases; they are there to protect horse populations as a whole.

6   **Infections** may be contracted while a horse is being ridden or at shows, race meetings or competitions; they have the most serious influences on racehorses.

7   **Infection** may become established in an individual horse because of poor stabling conditions and bad feeding, so causing a lowering of resistance.

8   **If your horse appears** to be infected, consult your vet about treatment; however, treatment of low-grade infections is often best achieved by providing wholesome food, comfortable stabling conditions and access to grass.

9   **The more intensive** the training, the greater the risk of infection, so the higher the standard of management required and the greater the degree of understanding needed from you.

10 **In serious disease outbreaks,** isolation and turning horses out is a help, as long as neighbouring horses are not put at risk.

11 **Infections** in a large yard may be mixed and run one after another, so there can be a long period of infection; this is best dealt with by dispersing horses.

12 **In specific conditions,** like EVA or EHV, the risk of spreading the infection may mean horses cannot be dispersed except within the limits of the infected unit.

7 | Pasture Management

For the horse, the changes from a life roaming wide ranges to one under domestic management has brought a whole variety of matters to consider. As we have seen, Nature's design of a perfection-requiring body could not always be met in the wild. Measured against this, domestication allowed for greater control of nutrition and provided protection from the more volatile aspects of the elements. But at what price?

MAN'S IMPOSED LIFESTYLE

One basic difference between free range living and domestication is that on the one hand, man has no influence, and on the other he has. Total control is, in fact, possible under many of today's systems of management, but this varies from the relative illusion of total freedom for the horse in the field, to the almost absolute control over the horse in training for competition or racing.

In the field, freedom is restricted by fences and gates, and the horse can never live its life without at some time being handled and fed by man. Furthermore, the very act of concentrating animals together brings inevitable worm infestation, along with other problems such as soiled areas, grazing scarcity and deficiency conditions. And it is seldom possible for herds to live in such isolation that they are protected from wind-borne infections or from all contact with outside sources.

Within modern yards, horses are often never out of human control except when they get rid of a rider and take off on their own. Otherwise they may well stay stabled for twenty-two hours out of every twenty-four, and everything they eat and drink is provided by their carers. While this means effective control of every detail, it is not a truth fully appreciated as yet. The construction and control of the stable, its environment, bedding, hygiene and feeding are all provided, and so can be used or changed as the situation dictates. Obviously man controls food, but it is also possible to control water quality, and to detect and remove almost any unwanted substance, as long as we know it is there.

What domestication means for most horses is an ordered existence. Against this there is a duty of performance that ranges from good manners to exercises

---

THE HORSE IN THE WILD

- Covers wider distances to obtain dietary variety.
- Has little or no contact with man, and may strongly resent any such contact.
- There are more entire horses, smaller family bands, and fewer mares per stallion.
- Is subject to the weather and growth/water conditions.
- Has very hard feet.
- Injured horses are exposed to predators.

involving the carrying of weight, including simple riding, driving, jumping under saddle, and maybe something as heavy as ploughing.

The essence of the human/horse relationship is cooperation, and while this is not always a willing reality, most horses give of themselves generously, and with only the very lightest of discipline. With the exclusion of those few who see their horses as a means of creating fame, or money, or both, the average horse enjoys a fulsome, rewarding and happy life at the hands of its owners today.

Domestication therefore means the horse is kept in fields that are subject to all that man can do to enhance, or more significantly, to harm them. Thus the nutritional status of the grasses is affected by the kind of seed mixtures that are sewn; the soil is influenced by the dressings added to it; and the edible herbage may be coated in dust from neighbouring industry, or drenched in rains that carry pollution from afar, or covered in lead from the exhausts of passing cars. In addition there may be worm eggs or larvae, the encysted cercariae of liver fluke, or even bacterial and viral organisms deposited by other horses. The water to the fields may arrive in lead pipes, or come from supplies heavily contaminated by the run-off from intensive farming, or have a high metallic content, leached from the soil by the acidity of the rain.

> ## THE HORSE IN DOMESTICATION
>
> ■ Experiences familiarity with man.
> ■ Has all food provided – but this leaves the door open to human error.
> ■ Stabling and shelter are provided where needed – but he is kept in confined paddocks.
> ■ Must work in return.
> ■ He is less hardy, has softer feet, and suffers more injuries; but he is nursed through illness and injury.
> ■ Is likely to be shod, submitted to harness, ridden.
> ■ Suffers more disease.

THE OUTDOOR ENVIRONMENT

If we take a worst-case scenario, accepting as true all the more serious warnings of the environmental groups, how can this be expected to affect the horse in the field? For the young and developing animal, any interference with daily nutrition, either through deficiencies, imbalances or the intake of toxic materials, has immediate implications for healthy growth, future soundness, as well as the capacity to attain full athletic ability at a later stage. For the already mature horse, it could mean interference with normal physiological processes and, therefore, reduced levels of performance and increased incidence of disease, be these performance-related or simply challenges to health. Nutritional conditions lead, as we know, to stunted growth, poor coat, and abnormal hoof development. They are prevented by recognising the root causes and taking steps to counter them.

The immediate problem arises from the quality of herbage affected by pollutants, weakened, possibly, by acidity affecting the soil. Thus, if we accept the findings of research mentioned elsewhere here, there is less protein and minerals on even artificially fertilised herbage when compared with that organically produced. The sources of water also have to be evaluated and the effects of water-borne toxins allowed for, as might the effects of altered climatic conditions due to environmental warming, or, alternatively, cooling, either of which might inhibit growth and, hence, nutrition.

Of course, when providing supplementary feeding to offset the effects of all this, it should be appreciated that even balanced diets will have no influence over toxic materials or already damaged tissues. Where such problems exist, the animal may only resume normal development, if at all, when removed to a clean source.

WINTER GRAZING

The environmental conditions in places like Ireland and New Zealand mean that horses are able to spend all four seasons at grass, and outwintering for even non-native types is often possible with only hay as a supplement. It works in Ireland because the climate is dictated mainly by westerly weather systems coming off the Atlantic. The weather is mild, if wet, and there are fewer periods of cold easterlies which, coming from the continent of Europe, hit the east coast of Britain first. Grass growth is lush, the growing season long, and there is usually a late as well as an early bite. Even so, many outwintered horses, especially in-foal mares, will need additional feeding.

In Britain, the longer and colder winters bring greater hardship for animals kept outdoors, and the rigours of the weather mean that most horses spend at least the colder and wetter nights indoors, or in field shelters; it is a measure of man's caring. In the Alps, horses spend the whole of each winter indoors, except when they are working, as the extremes of weather would never allow for anything else. But in more temperate climes, moorland ponies and other horses spend their lives in the open, exposed to the elements, usually without consequence. It therefore comes as a surprise to see, in other areas, long-haired horses dressed in rugs and hoods: and this makes little sense, since with full coats they should be as hardy as cattle, especially native breeds.

The outdoor horse in winter conditions may need supplementary feeding to survive

GRASS QUALITY

The quality of grass is of critical importance to a horse's growth and development, especially for those spending critical parts of their lives with little else as a source of nutrition. Most foals spend the whole of their first year at grass. In Thoroughbred breeding, weaning occurs in the autumn, but this is not the general practice with non-Thoroughbreds, where foals may run with their dams until the time comes for mares to go to stud again, and beyond.

There is no more natural feed than good grass

Flat-bred Thoroughbred yearlings are likely to spend their nights stabled and to run at grass during the day, at least as long as that practice remains a practical possibility. The limiting factors are temperament and the risk of injury, also vices that may, or may not, result in loss of condition. Flat-bred colts and fillies are generally produced for yearling sales, or enter training in the autumn of their yearling year without going to sales. Their diet will always be supplemented, especially from the time they are weaned; in fact the whole of their lives, from the very day they are born, is controlled to ensure that they meet their full growth potential. They are exercised in hand from early spring of their yearling year, and this is essentially the start of their training as athletes, when their outdoor life is mainly over. Ideally they are highly developed and physically hard when they go to a trainer's yard.

Horses bred to jump, on the other hand, generally spend the main part of their developing years at grass, until they are three or four, and the decision to supplement or balance their feed depends purely on physical development, the quality of the grass they eat, and the number of animals with which they have to compete for it. The more valuable horses – those that will have to establish their value at sales or in competition – generally get the benefit of the best grasses and the most careful supplementary feeding. However, the demands of commercial production may well mean that these very animals are the most challenged from a nutritional standpoint,by being over-fed; also the intensity of their stocking rates may lead to their being seriously disadvantaged as regards parasites and other forms of disease (especially as foals under their dams, when at stud).

Mature athletic horses have a requirement for crude protein at between 8 and 12 per cent of diet. This will vary upwards while they are actively growing, being at its highest for unweaned foals, whilst the maintenance requirement of mature, sedentary animals may be less. Where too much protein is given in the diet of any animal, the result may be abnormal growth and excessive fat deposit. Conversely, the effect of pushing pastures for horses may result in inadequate nutritional value, leading to poor development and mineral imbalances.

Moorland ponies and American mustangs get little help from anything other than Nature, but their own nature is adapted to allow for that. They are generally more weather-durable, and within certain limitations they are tougher than the domesticated horse: their feet are hardier; their bone, when adequately nourished and built, is strong. Most notably, they are not subjected to intensive training, but have a natural state of fitness that is measured against their needs of self-defence, the turmoil of breeding competition, and the demands of roaming far and wide in the search for food.

Cyclical Growth

The natural seasonal cycle means that grass growth tails off in autumn, winter being, in most areas, a time of minimal growth. Real growth starts in spring, but is slowed in summer during times of prolonged drought and excessive sunshine. The stores of fat laid down at times of profusion provide energy for animals during dry periods, though as a general rule, supplementation is needed during winter if horses are not to lose condition.

An additional consideration is the harm done to pastures by heavy poaching in wet seasons, and the effect this will have on subsequent grazing. A balance needs to be kept, and denuded areas need rest, replenishment, and perhaps reseeding before they can again become fertile.

The Dangers of Small Paddocks

The trend to smaller paddocks, or to increased stocking rates in larger ones, is unfortunate if you happen to be a horse. A widening interest in riding among the young means that commercial operators are obliged to increase numbers because of economic factors, and are often unable to maintain the same low grazing densities they previously favoured; this means that often horses are kept where they never would have been in the past.

The horse needs both exercise and nutrition, and very often this need for movement is met by turning it out. However, horses are 'trickle feeders', and those turned onto bare ground have nothing to satisfy the requirements of such a regime. In many such cases loose hay is provided – but when the hay is gone, the horses may take to eating fences, or the bark and leaves of trees or shrubs that lie within their grasp, some of which may be poisonous. Vices are often a horse's way of expressing his exasperation at restrictive management practices – although stable-walking is surely born more out of frustration than protest.

Thus the back-garden horse is often only provided with a bare patch on which to browse and get a mere suggestion of exercise. However, even this is conceivably better than being shut up in a stable the whole time, even though the area may become very poached and dirty.

The Problem of Worms

It is almost inevitable that more horses per acre/hectare will result in higher levels of worm infestation. It was originally expected that broad-spectrum anti-worming drugs would make worm-free grazing a realistic prospect, but this has not proved to be the case: instead there has been a shift in worm species, and the clinical disease picture has shifted with it. The problem has come with drug resistance, in that worm species that have always been effectively killed by wormers have been replaced by others that were previously not a problem; also the notion that it is possible to clear contamination (using wormers) from intensively grazed paddocks is, at best, fanciful.

The result is that small strongyles have replaced the more traditional, but effectively treated, large strongyles. *Cyathostomum*, a tiny worm that resides encysted in the wall of the intestine during the winter months and emerges in spring, is a major disease problem today, able to resist treatment with drugs because of its lifestyle habit of burrowing into the bowel wall and remaining there for months on end. It is capable of causing infestations of huge numerical proportions, and there is often acute clinical disease as the worms emerge en masse from the bowel in spring. And, inevitably, when this problem is resolved, as it will be, another will develop if we place all our hopes in drug use only.

Damage Caused by Worms The damage caused by worms varies from mild tissue inflammation to serious internal migrations through blood vessels and organs such as the liver and lungs; moreover there are specific clinical conditions – for instance aneurysm development, obstruction and acute diarrhoea – that might even end in the death of the horse. The problem is at its worst where pasture hygiene is poor and many horses graze too few acres; it is at its least troublesome where grazing densities are low, where rotational grazing is possible, and where pastures are rested. Infectious stages of worms are killed by exposure to direct sunlight and winter conditions; those that survive this are controlled by knowing their nature and preventing build-up on the land. This may require removal of dung on a regular basis, or by ingestion by non-affected hosts such as cattle and sheep.

Damage Caused by Wormers While some drugs, for example organophosphate wormers, are potentially toxic in themselves, the adverse effect of many worm doses begins when they are excreted in the faeces of treated animals. This is because they have the potential to kill insects and other organisms that are vital to the whole cycle of organic breakdown and plant growth; there is also the possibility that, when used widely, residues will find their way into watercourses, thus ending up in drinking water, or in rivers and the sea. An instance of the former threat is that it has recently been found that the lowly dung beetle is being wiped out since the advent of avermectins. One characteristic of the dung beetle is that it is the intermediate host of the gullet worm, which we can do without; otherwise, however, it assists in the breakdown of faeces, a vital function of life in pastureland. Other non-targeted species are also susceptible to these drugs and are killed, and this can even extend to birds, river and marine life.

Paddock Vacuums Small paddocks, therefore, not only mean a fall-off in grazing quality but an inevitable increase in worm contamination. The idea that horse pastures might have a regular vacuuming to remove

SOURCES OF WORMS

■ Some worm eggs over-winter and are the source of new season infections.

■ Intensively grazed paddocks may become worm sick.

■ Heavily infested new stock will contaminate clean pastures.

■ Some worms may be transmitted by intermediate hosts, such as snails, mites and beetles.

■ Others are left on scratching posts and railings, on feed buckets and in stables.

IMPORTANT POINTS IN WORMING

- Drug resistance makes worming a waste of time and money where the predominant worms are not killed.
- Expecting drugs to control potential worm problems on intensively grazed fields is impractical.
- Good medicine demands limiting contamination and minimising non-essential drug use; routine dosing is the opposite of this.
- Horses may develop immunity by constant low-level exposure.
- High-level infestation causes clinical conditions that might even result in death.
  Prevention is by good hygiene and an understanding of worm life-cycles and where to break them.

droppings has, as yet, seldom proved a practical proposition: removing them by hand is horribly labour intensive, yet the kind of machinery designed to serve the purpose was always likely to be used by only a minority of people. Yet the threat of worms is not going away, nor is the advent of new and more effective wormers anything about which we should be overjoyed, or indeed complacent.

Grazing for Horses in Training Owners whose horses compete and are never turned out to graze rest happy in the knowledge that their exposure to worm infestation is minimised. Yet there is a growing weight of (anecdotal) evidence that horses in training allowed a few hours at grass are healthier in themselves and less likely to be affected by diseases – mostly infections – that prove limiting. There is, of course, the risk of accident to athletic animals in full fitness that have excess energy to burn off; yet trainers who manage to overcome the difficulties invariably find that the horses in their care are much better for being turned out for a while. However, obviously worm control is critical for these animals, and by providing clean grazing rather than using drugs.

Grazing Habits Horses, as we know, tend to avoid grazing pasture they have soiled, and this leads to uneconomical grazing. Cattle and sheep that graze the same pasture will not be so discriminating, and horses, too, will graze right up to cattle or sheep faeces without showing the aversion they evidently have to their own. Note that harrowing only increases the potential worm burden, and is not a good idea on contaminated pastures, except as a prelude to resting or ploughing; this is because it breaks up and spreads droppings and exposes worm eggs and larvae over a wider area, making the land more infectious for any horse that grazes it in that state. Of course if the land is rested, exposure to the elements will kill off susceptible worms, although the more resistant might be unaffected.

Existing Worm Problems Where there is an existing problem the diagnosis is made through faecal analysis, and the laboratory may advise further tests; the drug of choice can be decided on the basis of the results. The organic ideal means avoiding wormers that might harm soil organisms when excreted from the horse, or that might leach through to be consumed by other species. It is also basic to this that routine procedures are aimed at eliminating dependence on wormers and that infection is kept down by good grazing practices.

Worms exposed to direct sunlight, that is, not protected in the herbage or dung pads, are soon killed, although there are known resistant types, such as the eggs of the

> ### TACKLING EXISTING WORM PROBLEMS
> ▪ Diagnosis is through faecal analysis.
> ▪ Seriously contaminated pastures may need to be ploughed.
> ▪ Harrowing breaks up dung pads and exposes larvae to the weather.
> ▪ Recently harrowed pastures should not be grazed as there is an increased risk of worm infection.
> ▪ There is a spring rise in the excretion of some worms, endangering clean pastures.
> ▪ Very contaminated pastures benefit from regular removal of faeces.
> ▪ Cross grazing with cattle and sheep helps reduce contamination for horses.

horse roundworm, *Parascaris*. The larvae of others are capable of surviving the chills of winter, such as the small strongyle, *Cyathostomum*, believed to have become significant because of a combination of resistance and the elimination of other types. These are released from the wall of the gut in large numbers in the spring, thus being capable of causing new problems on even previously clean pastures.

Ultimately, if the organic line is taken seriously, the steps to follow are the reduction of exposure to worms, the use of drugs only when clinically indicated (based on faecal analysis, perhaps, as well as physical condition), and only those drugs used that kill the specific problem and have no further implications relating to environmental toxicity. The idea is to make routine dosing a redundant exercise. Of course, the essence of worm reduction comes back to acceptable grazing densities, paddock resting, rotation with other species, and an understanding of worm cycles and how infection builds up.

Parascaris was effectively treated in the past using piperazine, which was cheap, virtually non-toxic, and not known to have any residual effect. This is a worm that responds to most common drugs today, but the problems it poses arise from the susceptibility of foals, that often harbour large numbers, the prolific egg-production of the females, and the resistance of those eggs to exposure on the land. It is possible that they can even survive ploughing and crop rotation, though they would have to be greatly diluted in the process. These, however, are the kind of details that need to be understood, and it is not possible to go through them all here.

The situation is complicated by worms like *Cyathostomum*, which is capable of infecting in large numbers and is resistant to many drugs when present in the wall of the gut, where it may remain through the winter before emerging and maturing. Where this worm becomes a problem, the answer has to include the use of an effective drug (there are several that claim to be) coupled with reduced grazing density, rotational grazing, and removal of faeces. The alternative is inevitable disease, the problem of ineffective drugs as resistance to them grows, and the unnecessary risk to the environment through their use.

FACTORS AFFECTING PASTURE QUALITY

The organic horse we envisage is still a man-made animal, based on all the conventions of domestication. We have total control over his growth and development, and he depends on us to maximise the potential of his physique and athleticism. Here we will consider his time at pasture – and he is fortunate in that we can provide with greater ease and certainty a quality of grazing that is sometimes elusive on the plains. Inevitably this depends on a number of factors: soil fertility, pH value, available minerals, levels of rainfall, temperature and land use.

Excessive acidity is countered by liming or the use of slag, the benefit of which was recorded by the Romans as early as the first century AD. While acidity may be affected by acid rain, there are many other factors involved. Most grasses, including the highly nutritious perennial ryegrass, do well in mineral soils at a pH of 6.0, and in peaty soils at pH 5.5. Liming neutralises excessively acid soils, thereby improving the structure and aiding the absorption of minerals by plants. Excessive acidity can lead to a deficiency of the trace elements iron, boron, copper and molybdenum, and it increases the availability of the potentially toxic metals aluminium and manganese, which adversely affect plant growth.

The Effects of Rain Heavy rainfall adversely affects soil acidity; in particular it leaches calcium from acid soils, and acid rain increases the effect. Surface acidity makes the roots more susceptible to damage through grazing, and also to drought. When subsoils become acid, the problem is more difficult to resolve, and ploughing may become necessary.

Pig slurry, like that being spread here, is high in copper. Acidification and nitrate levels may also be affected by slurry spreading

Slurry Cattle slurries that are rich in nitrogen and potash may also contribute to acidification and cause the leaching of nitrates. Nitrogen, phosphorus and potassium are the main nutrients in slurry, but calcium, magnesium, sulphur and trace elements are also present in valuable amounts; urine is rich in nitrogen and potassium; dung is rich in phosphorus, calcium, magnesium, sulphur and trace elements, although it needs to be decomposed for these to become available to the plants. Pig manure is high in copper; poultry manure is high in zinc.

Nitrogen Although it is a source of unwanted pollution (as nitrate or nitrite), nevertheless nitrogen is, as we have seen, the most important nutrient involved in grass production. Grass roots take up soil nitrogen (some of which comes from the air) mainly in the form of nitrate, though ammonium is also a source. In the plant, it is essential to the formation of amino acids and more complex proteins: through this process the leaves grow, and the essential process of photosynthesis is increased. This is the reaction that allows the formation of carbohydrates (from atmospheric carbon dioxide and water) in the green tissues of plants under the influence of light. It is, it might be said, one of the most important chemical processes of life, in that through it, the energy in plants is produced that, digested by animals, finds its way through the food chain and onto our own plates.

When nitrogen is deficient in soils the leaves of plants are pale and discoloured. Some nitrogen comes through rainfall, and a high percentage consumed in herbage is excreted again by the animals eating it.

GRASS TYPES

- Perennial and Italian ryegrass are of high nutritional value because of their digestibility and dry matter content. They are durable and tolerate heavy grazing, but are at a disadvantage in dry conditions or on infertile land, and do not like winter cold or frost during early spring growth.
- Timothy is weak in the face of intensive grazing, but does well on wet, peaty and heavy soils. It is also winter hardy, tolerates less fertile soils, and provides an early bite. It has a low mineral content and loses digestibility as it matures.
- Cocksfoot does well in light-textured soils in dry areas and is tolerant of drought. However, it can be of low nutritional value, and is not highly productive.
- Meadow fescue grows best in cool, moist conditions and has been used in mixtures with timothy and white clover.
- Tall fescue grows well in dry or wet conditions. Established swards show good early spring growth, being winter hardy, but this grass is slow to establish, low in digestibility, and grazing animals do not favour it. However, it is important in places such as Argentina and the southern USA as a grazing source.
- Prairie grass is a species of brome grass that grows best in dry conditions and shows a good autumn growth. It does well on free-draining soils under mild conditions where there is little frost. It is of good digestibility, and is liked by stock. Sweet brome has similar attributes, but is not used on any wide basis.

Legumes Atmospheric nitrogen is fixed by nodules that develop in the root systems of legumes and which are formed by interaction with bacteria in most soils. This makes the addition of clover species to seed mixtures an attractive benefit, in that it can reduce the amount of nitrogenous fertilisers used. White clover, a perennial legume, does not proliferate in soils with a pH of less than 5.8 or in those that are poorly drained; it is also sensitive to deficiencies of phosphorus, potassium or trace elements.

THE EFFECTS OF LIME USAGE

- Lime provides calcium which is essential for plant growth.
- Grasses contain 4–12gm/kg calcium in their dry matter.
- Legumes are sensitive to a deficiency of calcium, which affects their ability to fix nitrogen.
- Clay and peaty soils require more lime than sandy soils.
- Excessively heavy liming can limit the availability of phosphorus, manganese and boron to plants, thereby causing a deficiency in grazing animals.
- For quicker effect, farmers use nitrogenous fertilisers to stimulate plant growth. The immediate benefit may be offset as acidity increases, especially on mineral soils, but there is a price to pay in the way of nutritional quality.

SIGNS OF ACIDITY

- Yorkshire fog, red fescue and bent grasses predominate, and weeds such as sorrel and spurrey are common.
- The lower nutritional value of these is reflected in the reduced benefit they have for grazing animals.
- Perennial ryegrass and white clover growth suffer in these conditions.
- Earthworm acitivity and microbial breakdown are adversely affected, and material that would otherwise be digested may form a mat that inhibits plant growth.

Clovers have a high protein and a high sugar content, and a lot of clover in pastures for horses may lead to laminitis, excessive fat deposition, and defective bone in young horses. There is also a tendency to abnormal physical development – pot-bellies and stunted growth – in foals and yearlings, which may reflect abnormal hind-gut digestion through lack of fibre.

Lucerne is a favoured legume in horse feeding because of its protein and calcium content, and because it has a beneficial influence on energy digestion. Birdsfoot trefoil is common in Canada and north-eastern USA where it thrives in the humid conditions; it is also used on wetland pastures in New Zealand and Australia.

Secondary Grasses These consist of bent grasses, fine-leaved fescues, Yorkshire fog, smooth and rough-stalked meadow grasses, crested dogstail and sweet vernal. They are generally not sown specifically, and are therefore called 'natural' or 'weed grasses'. They cover 25 per cent of the ground in 8 per cent of one- to four-year-old swards, a proportion which increases to 57 per cent after twenty years. They can be rich sources of crude protein where soil fertility is high, but are poorly digested, though with a high mineral content.

Yorkshire fog is prone to winter damage, and is not liked by stock when it is mature; however, it is digestible, a good source of minerals, and it responds well to fertilisers.

Good-quality hay may have a crude protein content as high as 15 per cent, although protein content may be as low as 5 per cent. It is therefore important to know the value of the hay you feed, and when it is being fed to competition horses, analysis is important if deficiencies are to be avoided.

LOOKING AT PASTURE MANAGEMENT

1 **When assessing** stocking rates consider grass quality, stage of growth, degree of poaching, and the extent to which land has been grazed.

2 **It is estimated** that 1 hectare (2.47 acres) of good grassland should provide grass and hay for three to four light horses; but there are no hard and fast rules, and the acreage per horse under organic conditions should ideally exceed this.

3 **Be aware** of the stage of growth of your pasture; it may be necessary to introduce cattle or sheep if there is too much grass for your horses.

4 **Remember** lush young grasses may predispose to laminitis in susceptible animals – which can include all types.

5 **Where land is intensively grazed,** horses should be moved on regularly to clean fields and the soiled land rested, perhaps harrowed to expose worms, and mixed grazing practised.

6 **The only form of fertiliser** used on organically produced grassland should be well-rotted farmyard manure.

7 **Remember** that the food value of the grasses in small paddocks is limited and the incidence of worms is magnified.

8 **Use common sense** when it comes to worm control; aim for a significant reduction on modern tendencies to wormer useage.

9 **Aim to reduce** the worm burdens of adult animals and limit reinfection by good grazing practice and clean pasture policies.

10 **At times** the use of wormers may be unavoidable, but the idea is to reduce dependency and disprove the idea that routine worming is an essential tool of horse management.

11 **Wormers** are used where critical illness from worms is evident.

12 **The use of** regular dung analysis is useful in trying to achieve an organic approach to worm control.

Water Quality

The idea of producing an organic horse meets its greatest difficulty when facing the problem of water quality. Only in areas of the planet untouched by man would it be possible to breed and rear him in optimum organic conditions, and there are few such places. Pollution is carried on the rain and wind, and spreads with the weather systems. It is plucked from its sources and taken to the widest corners; it covers innocent lands, drains into groundwater, and comes up in bore holes.

There is little chance of escaping its compass, especially as agriculture also contributes an array of chemicals; these alone percolate all the way through the food chain to Arctic animals and deep-sea fish. It is as if we are trying to test Nature to the very limits of her tolerance. Ideally the organic horse should be free of any of this. His sire and dam should be as perfect as it is hoped they will produce their foal. Their food sources should be abundant and chemical free. The sire must produce vigorous and healthy semen, with no external factors diminishing his sperm count or making any of them physically abnormal. The mare must be provided with the stimulus to produce a single fertile ovum; her rich hormones should make her receptive, and clean the womb for an uncomplicated pregnancy that will develop a healthy foal free of infection and fully grown. Nothing in their surrounds must hinder it. Is this an unattainable dream?

WHERE DOES WATER COME FROM?

Water is a compound of hydrogen and oxygen that forms abundantly in the atmosphere and is essential to all known forms of life on Earth. More than 97 per cent of free water is salty, and 99.5 per cent of the remainder is locked away in icecaps and glaciers. Of the 500,000 cubic kilometres of sea water evaporated each year by the sun, about 40,000 drifts onto land as new, usable water; almost two thirds of this is lost in floods or held in soil and swamps, leaving about 14,000 cubic kilometres to remain for man's use.

Viruses and bacteria enter water from ground sources; coliforms are a sign of faecal pollution. Selenium and arsenic occur in various rock strata and may be found in deep rock wells. Chromium may cause kidney damage, as also may cadmium.

COMMON ADDITIVES

Chlorine Used in dilute solution, chlorine is universally used to kill organisms in water. Bacterial contamination is measured by culturing or counting coliform numbers (organisms that generally have a faecal origin, either human or animal). Consideration is generally not given to the prospect that some organisms might be chlorine resistant. This possibility increases with resistant viruses, with organisms such as cause BSE in cattle, and protozoal organisms such as *Cryptosporidium*, of animal origin and blamed for frequent outbreaks of human gastroenteritis from water sources.

Chlorine can also interact with humic acid and other natural debris in water to produce toxic cancer-causing substances; it can also combine with phenols to form chlorophenols which make water taste like TCP. It may, however, combine with ammonia to form chloramines, which bond chlorine and prevent these unwanted reactions. But if the ratio of chlorine to ammonia is wrong, then dichloramines may be formed, which are foul-tasting and may generate nitrites.

As already mentioned, a 1977 survey found that people in New York counties drinking chlorinated water suffered a 44 per cent higher death rate from gastrointestinal and urinary tract cancers than those that did not. Chlorine is also capable of causing skin irritation and increasing urine production (diuretic).

Aluminium The dangers of aluminium in water were especially highlighted in the poisoning of a whole district in Cornwall, England, some ten years ago. It is an element with many uses – for instance, aluminium hydroxide is a common antacid used in human gastric ulcers. However, its potential toxic influences are a real concern, not least its capacity to deposit in bone and brain tissue within the body, where it can cause brittle bones, anaemia and brain disease.

Fluoride This is the generic name for salts of the gas fluorine. While widely used for its ability to prevent dental disease, it has also been found to cause mottling and discoloration of teeth. It has been implicated in injury to the brain and nervous system, also in bone deformity, arthritis, allergies, duodenal ulcers, cancer and diabetes. It is also thought to be a factor in goitre, personality disorders and kidney failure. Initially it was added as sodium fluoride – a rat poison – to water. A medical survey carried out in 1985 concluded that fluoride damages enzyme systems and DNA. Mouth ulcers, stomach and bowel disorders, cramps and diarrhoea have all been linked to fluoridated toothpaste.

Fluoride can occur naturally in water and has been associated with bone deformity in parts of India, and with black teeth in volcanic regions.

SUBSTANCES FOUND IN WATER

- Aluminium, calcium (causes hardness), iron, magnesium (also causes hardness), manganese, sodium, fluoride, selenium, chromium, cadmium, copper, mercury, lead, silver.
- Chlorides and sulphates.
- Hydrogen sulphide, sometimes present as a gas.
- Nitrate nitrogen.
- The residues of herbicides, pesticides, fungicides and fertilisers.
- Other effluents such as silage liquor, slurry and sewage.

CHEMICALS USED TO TREAT WATER

- Chlorine, aluminium sulphate and fluoride are the most common.
- Also ferric sulphate, polaluminium chloride, sodium aluminate, polyelectrolytes.
- Sulphur dioxide and sodium thiosulphate, used to reduce chlorine levels.
- Ammonia and sodium hypochlorite, used for disinfection.
- Lime, soda ash, caustic soda and sulphuric acid, all used for pH adjustment.
- Calgon, used to soften water.

Water, the Conveyor of Compromising Substances Happily, society is becoming increasingly aware that drinking water can be the conveyor of unwanted substances, ranging from the extremes of poor hygiene seen in Third World regions where 25 per cent of children may die from water-borne infections, to the less visible problems of more advanced but densely populated countries. This latter ranges from the toxicity of corroding metal pipes to the chemicals leaching from farmland, and the outpourings of industry. Infections may be transmitted, as just mentioned. And we must consider other poisons that might fall outside the range of the usual expected parameters, as happened after Chernobyl.

For the horse, this may mean greater problems than already come in his feed. Whether his water is piped from a private well or stream, or is collected rainwater, there is a considerable possibility of his being exposed to substances which are harmful. And although this may have little evident effect on the sedentary life he enjoys in a field, it could limit the athletic ability of a more active animal, or could influence the capacity to deal with low-grade disease. It could also, of course, affect longevity.

The dangers are highlighted by work reported in the *New Scientist* in 1998, which found that pesticide chemicals and tin-can lacquers were able to influence the hormonal

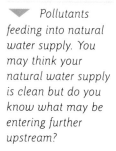
Pollutants feeding into natural water supply. You may think your natural water supply is clean but do you know what may be entering further upstream?

output of the pituitary glands of rats, an eventuality which might then lead to sexual changes and fertility problems. The same thinking aligns these and similar substances to falling human sperm counts. Science has also established that PCBs – used, for example, in flame retardants and in the cleaning of nuclear submarines – collect in polar bear fat, and are thought to cause an increasing incidence of hermaphroditism among this species. The same chemicals are recognised to be toxic to humans and animals, causing damage to the liver and it is thought to the central nervous system. They have found their way into rivers and seas: seals, cetaceans and other marine mammals in their native regions have all been found to have high levels in their fat, and experimental poisoning has led to diarrhoea, poor weight gain and abortion. They are said to have caused 80 per cent sterility in North Sea seals, and to have reduced disease resistance in a manner that allowed a distemper-like virus to cause serious losses in the late eighties.

Were the developmental and reproductive elements of this to be applicable to horses, inevitably the problems for geldings would be least serious. Fertility in mares is at best a variable entity, as we will see later, and it does not need a great deal of environmental disruption to affect it; moreover it would seem that all the modern advances in veterinary technology have done little to improve the situation. It remains subject to such simple factors as season, daylight time and nutrition as well as other climate-related factors.

Also implicated are substances like DDT (an insecticide), phthalates from food packaging, and TBT, the ship anti-fouling paint. From our point of view, what is not measured is the degree to which such toxic materials might exist within a competing horse, and to what extent their presence might inhibit expression of his full talent. This, of course, is quite apart from any implications regarding his health, disease resistance, or indeed longevity. But we must take it that the potential exists, as the horse in the field is surely as exposed as the bear at the Pole.

THE EFFECT ON THE HORSE

While it has to be accepted that the vast bulk of water consumed meets the standards set by national and international authorities, the question arises as to how mainly low level quantities of unwanted materials might affect the growth and development, even the very future of an animal species. How might they intrude on the working of normal processes within the body, and how might this predispose to disease? The demands of that perfectionist, Nature, are likely to be impeded when such substances adversely affect digestion, disturb mineral balances, and impair the normal working of the liver.

The Pathways of Pollution The pathways of pollution are well documented, from sources that begin in industry and agriculture. From industry, toxins gain access to rivers, seas and water courses by means of liquid discharges; they are also carried from smoke emissions through wind and clouds, and fall with the rain.

Agricultural pollutants are leached under different conditions. They may be washed through by the rain, or dissolved through chemical processes, as when the rain itself is acidic. The road back to the horse is through his drinking water.

Aerial spraying of lime into a dying lake in Sweden to counter acidification

The Effects of Acid Rain

Acid rain was first recognised in 1872 as a consequence of factory effluent causing damage to local vegetation. The problem has since been found on a very wide basis, causing ecological damage to mountain forests, rivers and lakes, killing trees and other vegetation, and destroying fish and wildlife. The main substances involved are sulphur dioxide and nitrogen oxides, both of which may enter the atmosphere naturally, as a result of volcanoes or fires.

However, man-made releases from the smokestacks of coal or oil-fired power stations and factories are commonly responsible nowadays, and vehicle emissions have added hugely to this contribution in the latter half of the past century. Hydrocarbons, released from fossil fuels, are also to blame, as well as gases such as hydrogen fluoride.

While water acidity may be a natural phenomenon in particular areas due to soil types and rock structures, the more serious man-made acidity is caused by environmental pollutants. On occasion this may lead to acid precipitate falling at long distances from the source of pollution; in some cases, there may even be a visible element to this, as happened one day in a racing yard in Berkshire, where the ground was littered with red metallic particles after a shower.

When acid rain soaks into land it can cause metals such as aluminium, mercury, manganese, lead and zinc to leach into the water supply, and inevitably this creates toxic problems for those consuming it, including any horses. Innumerable sources advise of the environmental damage caused by acid rain, proposing that it can destroy the essential nutritive systems of vegetation. Furthermore the contamination of drinking water with metals may be the cause of overt disease, such as inflammation of the bowel, leading to mineral imbalances. And as a progression from this, it may also affect disease resistance and contribute to the problems of low-grade infection.

Remembering again the idealist in Nature, the equine digestive system was designed to consume water that was not tissue corrosive and that did not adversely affect the working of digestive enzymes by altering stomach and bowel pH. While there is no scientific evidence to support such a contention, the possibility has to exist. Humans confronted with bad-tasting drinking water have the means of rejecting and replacing it, but horses do not have that option and are obliged to take what comes in order to slake their thirst.

The pH of rain can fall to less than 3.0; at such levels it will kill fish and contaminate water supplies with heavy metals. Aluminium toxicity peaks at pH 5, and acid rain also leaches potassium, magnesium and calcium from soils, which may interfere with

ACID RAIN

- Up to 60 per cent of acidity is caused by sulphuric acid, less by nitric acid and a smaller amount due to hydrochloric acid.
- Rainfall is naturally acidic with a pH of around 5.6, but this may be brought down where pollution levels are high.
- Power stations and heavy smelting industries – lead, iron, steel, copper and aluminium – cause all sulphur and most nitrogen oxide emissions.
- Vehicle exhaust emissions are highly significant.
- Hydrogen fluoride is thought to be implicated.
- Ozone is known to damage leafy vegetables, crops and trees.

the nutrition of trees. Natural rainwater may be slightly acidic due to absorption of carbon dioxide while falling. Rain from polluted air over North America and northern Britain averages between 5.1 and 4.1. The lowest pH of rain recorded in Britain was 2.4 at Pitlochry, in Scotland.

Rainwater that is already acid may absorb more carbon dioxide if it passes through decaying vegetation. The carbon dioxide may turn to carbonic acid, which can be actively corrosive; if it then passes through rock, such as granite, the acidity is unchanged, and may be able to strip the lining of lead pipes. Acid water may, however, be treated by passing it through a tank of limestone chips, or a solution of sodium carbonate may be added to neutralise it. Acidified lakes are usually clear and lifeless.

The Acidification of Soils This occurs slowly as a natural process, is greatly quickened by acid rain, and is considered to destroy essential fungi that are vital to the growth of trees as well as other plants. It is also a known consequence of intensive crop production. It is blamed for the release of poisonous quantities of aluminium, and other metals, into watercourses. So what does this mean to the horse? We have already seen that soil acidity affects plant growth and nutritional quality. The use of soluble nitrogenous fertilisers is one example of how it could happen; the gradual influence of intensive farming methods on vegetable quality, according to Schuphan in 1975, was to lower yields by almost a quarter. Organically grown produce also had higher dry matter, protein, sugar, calcium, phosphorus, potassium and iron. Various research projects tend to support the view that this improvement

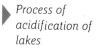

Process of acidification of lakes

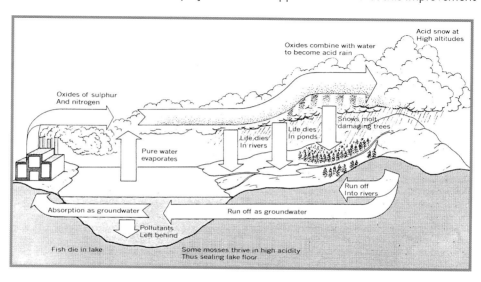

in quality of organic food directly relates through to growth and fertility, and although it cannot be said that this is conclusive, the balance of probabilities is favourable.

Pesticides in Water There is still a great deal of research to be done into the pathological effects of pesticides, but they have been detected in diverse areas and species, and this in itself is an ongoing ecological concern. The associated changes in sexual development and fertility problems, widely commented on, is a warning we cannot ignore; and the effects on disease resistance in the offspring of affected animals and the disturbance to lower life forms, is added evidence that should highlight the urgency of control measures.

The Robens Institute at Surrey University recently found evidence of over 300 chemicals in local tap water, to include pesticides, herbicides, industrial solvents, also traces of contraceptive pills, Valium, Mogadon and aspirin.

Metals in Water The tissue-corrosive properties of heavy metals means that, even in dilute amounts, there is a capacity to cause local tissue damage after consumption. The immediate effect of this may be no more than mild abdominal pain which will go undetected, but the propensity exists for the chemical disruption of digestion and consequent mineral imbalances and disease.

Tap Water This is capable of containing toxic chemicals and heavy metals from industrial processes, nitrates and pesticides from farming, and bacteria and phosphates from inadequately treated sewage. Lead is also a problem, as is cadmium and aluminium. *Cryptosporidium* organisms (from animal sources) have also become a problem in numerous supplies, and are thought to be chlorine resistant.

The Effect of Foreign Chemicals on Body Water Any associated problem is likely to be far more significant for the athletic horse than for any other, except perhaps the in-foal mare needing balanced mineral metabolism to produce a healthy offspring.

Any foreign chemical will have to be either excreted in the faeces, or, if it enters the bloodstream, neutralised in the liver or eliminated through the kidneys. While the first of these possibilities is the most ideal and only bears the threat of local tissue damage (if excretion is fully effective), entry to the body systems is an altogether more serious threat. Aluminium, as we have seen, concentrates in bone and nervous tissue and is very unwelcome there. Fluoride is capable of causing kidney damage at toxic levels. Inevitably, where critical safe levels are exceeded, toxicity is in prospect. Individual tolerance levels may vary between animals, meaning the effect of even low-level doses is greater for one animal than for another.

HYDRATION IN THE HORSE

There are, essentially, three water compartments within the body: the cells, the blood vascular system, and the area between these two, which is the conduit for substances passing in either direction between the other compartments. Water within the cells accounts for about 70 per cent of total body water; less than 10 per cent exists in the blood vascular system, and the balance comes in between. There is also a sizeable volume of water within the digestive system at times, varying with the stage of digestion and the volume of food in the gut. The significance of this latter detail to a racing animal might be the difference between a good performance and running badly. It is often said that one way to stop a racehorse is to make him drink a bucket of water before going onto the track. It is also felt that horses sweating excessively before a race will dehydrate and run badly, though there have been some notable exceptions to this. Whether or not dehydration will adversely affect peformance depends on degree. Some loss can be made up by absorption from the bowel, in which case the time interval between sweating and competing would be a factor. Also, many horses that boil over before racing are clinically sick anyway, and never were going to run up to their ability at the time.

Dehydration Water is lost from the body in urine, faeces, and through insensible loss (sweating and breathing); it is also lost in vomiting and diarrhoea. Dehydration is marked externally by a dry coat that is tightly attached to underlying tissues: the skin over the neck and abdomen can be picked up, and the elasticity – or lack of it – that it displays is a measure of this. Tightness is a reflection of fluid loss, and is not always noticeable in the early stages of the problem.

The quality of drinking water is critical. Remember even clear tapwater may contain unwanted substances

Loss of water from within the blood vascular system is more significant to performance because the consequent thickening of the blood adversely affects the pumping power of the heart, so hastening fatigue; too little oxygen then reaches tissues such as muscle, for example.

On laboratory analysis, dehydration of a healthy competing animal is most simply measured by packed cell volume (PCV). This is the measure of red cells against the total blood column, when spun in a centrifuge or allowed to stand long enough for the cells to settle. In normal circumstances, in a fit and healthy animal, equine PCV rests between 40–42 per cent (measured on blood taken when the animal is at rest and unexcited). Any deviation from the animal's normal level (estimated on regular checks and quantified against working standards) can be significant, and make the difference between success and failure. However, it must be kept in mind that fluid loss also occurs due to fever (from infection), and the change in PCV in this case will signify problems other than simple fluid and electrolyte loss. Higher PCVs can be compatible with performance in drugged animals or in those given red cells (illegally) as a means to artificially improving performance. The use of erythropoetin (EPO) in human athletes can lead to very high PCVs, and there is a recognised risk to life because of the altered fluid balance and the strain placed on the heart. The same, quite naturally, applies to the horse, where both blood doping and EPO use have been known in modern times.

It has been estimated that, in a healthy horse, as much as 7kg of water is lost when it is at grass on a moderate summer's day, without the coat showing any sign of sweat. This can be doubled in an hour when the same horse is working – the equivalent to 3 per cent of bodyweight to a 500kg horse (whose body will contain 350 litres of water). If double this quantity is lost, even over a period of days, the eyes will be sunken and the surface membranes dry.

Dehydration due to sweating not only means the loss of body fluid, but of electrolytes as well. Horse sweat also contains as much as 15gm of protein per litre (which makes it thick and may give it a soapy appearance). Sodium, potassium and chloride are all lost in sweat, and each is a factor in the fluid balance between body compartments. Potassium is most significant within the cells, and sodium and chloride are very important in the blood.

These are known criteria for the normal horse and are catered for today by the use of balanced electrolytes, as mentioned before, where these are considered necessary; however, this should allow for the fact that a balanced diet contains adequate quantities of electrolytes for all but heavy losses. The situation becomes more complicated where foreign chemicals disturb electrolyte balances or alter fluid levels, perhaps by promoting extra urine flow.

REMEDIES FOR WATER POLLUTION

There are filtering systems available to remove virtually any known substance from water. Some of these might be prohibitively expensive for the normal person; others are impractical because they quickly become saturated with the unwanted substance and are hence ineffective. Some denature the water and remove important minerals such as calcium and magnesium. Water can be purified by distillation, but it loses minerals in the process; it can be done by osmosis across semipermeable membranes, which is generally expensive; or contaminants can be extracted by chemical filters.

The important thing is to know what the contaminants are, when there is a problem, and to take expert advice on how to counter them. Of course in the end, the ideal would be for pollution to be eliminated and then there would be no problem. However, pollutants are often clearly to be seen, they are a possible health hazard, and should never be ignored. Thus, scum on stagnant water may contain organisms; water drunk from the edges of ponds may be a source of liver fluke, a problem likely to be increased in wet seasons; and any discoloration from rain could mean toxic levels of noxious chemicals. Heavily chlorinated water is bad tasting as well as unhealthy.

If your horse refuses to drink water, he may be trying to tell you something about its quality.

THE PROVISION OF WATER

1 **Domestic water supplies,** especially in heavily populated countries, are a source of many contaminants.

2 **Be aware** that even where horses are drinking from natural supplies, the possibility of contamination from industrial sources is high; contamination can also result from intensive farming as well as from the individual characteristics of local terrain.

3 **Water analysis** is, to an extent, an imprecise laboratory service; while most contaminants can be identified, there is such a wide variety that it may be impossible to identify an individual toxin causing a specific problem.

4 **Nitrate levels** are widely in excess of tolerance for competing animals and should always be an early consideration; filters are available to remove them.

5 **Acidity** is such a serious factor that horses may not drink affected water.

6 **It is also probable** that consumed acid water will affect metabolism; it may also carry heavy metals, compounding the effect.

7 **Chlorine** is considered to have clinical effects in humans; leaving it to stand might reduce levels by evaporation from the surface, though an effective filtering system is preferable, if costly.

8 **Fluoride** is a known human toxin and should not be added to any domestic water supply.

9 **Collected rainwater** may be heavily contaminated from industrial sources.

10 **Even virgin wells** may contain contaminants from intensive farming as well as the wash from acid rain.

11 **Comprehensive** filtering systems are available, though expensive for the average owner.

9 The Stable Environment

The importance of stabling to the organic horse is the significance of the part it plays in the creation, dissemination or control of disease. Science tells us that various types of worm can be transmitted through being deposited on doors, feed vessels, scratching posts and the like; also the incidence of allergies rises as we concentrate the causes in restricted and enclosed spaces. However, it is in the generation and spread of bacterial and viral diseases that the indoor existence is most influential. The secret of successful management is to understand what this means, to recognise the differences between an outdoor and an indoor existence, and to know which aspects favour infection, and which might counter it.

Writing in the middle of the nineteenth century, W. J. Miles, MRCVSL, remarked: '... stabling the horse is primarily a deviation from nature ... it often paves the way to disorders unknown, or varying in character from those of the animal in its aboriginal state.' At that time, horses working in cities and rural societies were a vital part of social and economic life. Remember, there were 300,000 horses working in London alone in 1890; and 1.3 million on farms in England and Wales in 1903. There were also 256,000 mules, jennets and asses in Ireland in 1900, as well as 259,761 horses classified as for agricultural purposes; in New Zealand, against a population of a million people in 1911, there were 404,284 horses; and this at a time when the official USA figure for horses exceeded 21.5 million.

All this meant a variety of types and breeds we do not see today. The Suffolk Punch, for example, once one of the predominant heavy horse types in Britain, had only a handful of foals registered in the early sixties, and is still only slowly being saved from extinction. The lighter Irish Draught was regenerated because it was such a useful producer of half-bred riding and jumping stock. Mules, jennets and asses in Ireland have dropped to a figure of about 8,000; in the USA in 1982, the number of mules had dropped

The Irish Draught is an important source of sound performance horses

The Suffolk Punch, no longer used extensively, is only being saved from extinction by caring people

to 27,000 from an all-time high of 5.9 million in 1925. It is hard to find much indication of leisure horse numbers at the turn of the last century; the only figures available are those provided by the Central Statistics Office in Ireland, whose records show about 20–25,000 horses and ponies for Amusement and Recreation, or about 5 per cent of all horses on average between 1861 and 1921. This figure might well be representative of other countries at the time, though it will have increased hugely today. It would have included hunters, and riding and competition horses, and there was also, of course, a significant population of military horses.

All this meant a range of management styles and a variety of stabling types. The farmer kept his horse perhaps tethered in a multi-purpose building, in stalls or in loose-boxes near cattle and other stock; the main reasons were convenience and cleanliness, so horses were easier to catch and to feed, and to provide them with some protection from inclement weather. There was also a need for stabling when there was no land and when the prospect of a run at grass was simply impossible, especially where large numbers were kept; typically this was in remount depots, merchants' yards and the like. The racehorse, Miles tells us, was catered for in those times with greater care and in high standards of warmth and comfort (which we have mostly found it convenient to dispense with today). The extent of this comfort is epitomised in the paintings of artists such as Stubbs and Herring, and is detailed in books like that of Miles, books which recorded the fashions and anecdotal opinions of the times.

It might be appropriate to mention again here the huge horse populations in those days relative to humans (in the USA, New Zealand and Ireland, approximately one horse to two or three people). This would certainly have generated its own intimate knowledge through familiarity and observation – by comparison, our opportunities today are minute when you consider that now there is one horse per forty–fifty people in the same countries, and one to one hundred in the UK; and it is therefore all the more surprising that we should so easily dispense with their accumulated wisdom, quite often without any proven reason to do so.

The more serious disease outbreaks occurred where horses were kept in large numbers, where their use was mostly commercial, and care was more functional than caring. We are led to believe that some of these places were unhygienic, foul-smelling and thoroughly unhealthy. The understanding of bacteria – how they caused disease, and how they spread – was primitive; medicine itself was only slowly evolving. Disease came from overcrowding, dirt and poor building design. The thinking person then, as now, had to see through the causes and learn how to avoid them.

WHY HAVE STABLES?

It needs to be appreciated that an indoor and an outdoor life for horses are entirely different entities, and good management has to treat them as such. The horse in the field has complete freedom of movement so that its circulation is constantly stimulated as it moves about, whereas most stabled horses have only limited space, if any, to move in – and 'too much' movement is thought to amount to a vice. The daily time at exercise for the latter is therefore the only stimulus it has for generating body heat, and the only assistance that it receives for the natural physiological processes that sustain health and fight off disease. Moreover, for every hour that it stands inside, it is at the mercy of the stabling conditions: thus if there are construction faults that favour disease, there is little chance of escape. In other words, if a horse finds its stable uncomfortable, it cannot complain or bring the matter to the notice of its carers. It is at such times that defences fail and diseases thrive, especially if there is significant variation in day- and night-time conditions, and if the influences of this are not prevented from having a direct effect on the horse.

THE OUTDOOR HORSE

The long-haired outdoor horse has the benefit of nature's protection to keep it warm. It is generally not in training: if it were, its groom would have the problem of coping with a dirty coat and copious sweating; moreover the lack of control over its diet, because of the amount and varying quality of grass eaten, would make condition and energy less easy to monitor. Feet would be softened if there were wet underfoot conditions; shoes lost. Worms would be more likely to infect it, and other diseases nearly as likely to occur as were the animal indoors.

▼ *Sporthorse youngsters running free – they are kept healthy by good management*

Field shelters provide useful winter cover

The clipped horse that runs outside will usually wear a heavy weatherproof rug (in appropriate conditions) and be brought in – though not always – at night. In New Zealand, in particular, it has been commonplace to train horses from the field, and this routine has been followed with limited success in Britain and Ireland. More commonly – conditions allowing – trained horses are now turned out during the day and stabled by night. The choice is between clean or muddy coats, and often between more or less infection – in short, the horse allowed to run outside will be healthier, although this must be measured against the risk of accident to highly fed and playful, fit animals. Also it must be said that the risk of infection outdoors increases if the horse stands about, gets wet, or is exposed to extremes of weather. On the other hand, a proper understanding of the requirements of stabled horses will lead to less infection, even without being turned out, if all the criteria that favour disease are recognised and avoided.

THE INDOOR HORSE

Stalls are rarely used today: horses have to be permanently tied up and seem reluctant to lie down – not an ideal situation

Various views are expressed relating to the indoor needs of horses, though little allowance is made for different uses and for the special needs of the athletic animal. Questions are raised about the significance of a hairy coat, and about the health status of animals living in the wild. However, while these points are not beyond argument, they do not apply directly to the horse kept indoors; the most obvious reason is clipping, which is done not only for convenience and cleanlinesss, but because of sweating, and its effect on hydration (as well as to avoid the problems of cleaning and drying). But we use rugs to compensate for hair, after which the most important difference between the horse in the wild and the horse envisaged here is the way we use him.

Athletic horses that are pushed to the limit in training are, as we have already seen, likely to be more susceptible to infection, just as the human endurance athlete is. For the horse, however, we have changed the ground rules, since we are no longer looking to convert food into physical strength only, but want speed, and the athleticism and

capacity to jump. Above all, we place demands on the respiratory system that cannot be answered in the presence of disease.

The athletic animal has a different set of priorities from the draught or cab-horse, both of which could cope with work while suffering mild infections. The racehorse, and to a lesser extent the eventer, can seldom tolerate these at all. They are asked to express themselves in peaks of physical achievement, either galloping, or jumping, or both; and to satisfy these demands they need to be at a peak of good health and condition. If they are carrying infection they may well be short of their best weight, and their body systems may be affected by the influences of fever and dehydration, or by alterations in the blood and by the release of enzymes that go with cell destruction. If they are cold, even if they are not infected, they may be obliged to burn off essential energy in order to sustain body heat – and this influence may drain their energy stores, and be the start of a downward spiral that ends in their being unable to withstand training. If they are too warm, of course, that could be equally harmful, though it is not a problem commonly met with today in temperate conditions.

 (top) Barn-type stable complex and (below) stallion barn in USA. Internal stabling such as this provides a constant temperate atmosphere and dry surroundings

It does not follow from this that all horses kept in unsuitable conditions will inevitably become infected. They do, however, become so more frequently, and they have greater problems recovering than those that are not. Moreover if they are constantly exposed to other horses – in competition, for example – they are more likely to keep picking up infections, and this will make it look as if they are always sick. This is because their resistance is lowered, and a constant supply of fresh organisms can set up serial episodes of disease: the horse is 'wrong', so it succumbs to sickness.

Be it empirical or not, people like Miles build a case for high ambient temperature requirements for stabled horses. Most modern sources, while giving lip-service to his stand, emphasise the need for air exchange and ventilation (which he also understood), and maintain that these outweigh all other considerations. Advice is variable, even contradictory, and tends to cover all animals, failing to appreciate the special requirements of maximally trained horses.

There is also a belief that chronic allergic respiratory disease is the most common and the most limiting problem affecting stabled horses; however, this is incorrect, and it is infection that is the most serious problem. If this becomes chronic, allergic conditions become more significant, and bleeding from the lungs frequently ensues. Bleeding, a limiting problem for racehorses, is nearly always preceded by detectable lung damage; but to suggest that all stabled horses should be kept in conditions suitable for allergy sufferers, or bleeders, is poor logic for the majority that have no such problems.

The basis of the 'fresh air' idea has also emerged from intensive stud farm management, where obviously the animals are not in training and are in tune with nature (at grass, mostly, and not clipped). Broodmares may well be healthier out of doors than when stabled – but again, it is a matter of degree, because most systemic infections do not interfere with fertility (unless, of course, they cause abortion). They might be healthier in highly ventilated barns than in stuffy conditions that saturate the air with infection, but they have a different set of needs from athletic horses, and they do have their own range of health problems.

Draughts in Stables Old literature is consistent in condemning the influence of draughts in stables, and no voice today is heard disputing this. However, there appears to be little understanding of what a draught is, and how it might affect disease resistance and health. We have no doubt what it is when gauging the effects for ourselves – in fact, we closet our bodies in such warmth (especially at home in our well insulated rooms) that we sometimes even endanger life itself: people have been known to die in atmospheres drained of oxygen. But exactly what is a draught that might have clinical effects for a horse, and what is not, and who can measure it? No research data exists to help us, and the answer – albeit subjective – is that if you can feel it and find it uncomfortable, then so will the horse; and if you, the groom or owner, feel cold in a stable, then the horse is likely to, too. The horse does not wish for the heat that we like when sitting by our fires, but it does like to be able to retain the heat it generates without being made too warm, and it likes clean air that is not saturated with urine smells, or is damp from cold walls or uninsulated floors. It also prefers to be moderately covered – it does not like to be made to sweat beneath too many rugs and duvets: it would rather have a warm building and fewer rugs than a cold building and heavier rugs that still may not keep it warm. Note that a horse that is so heavily rugged that it is on the verge of sweating, but whose legs, face and ears are cold, is almost certainly a sick horse.

FACTORS AFFECTING THE WELL-BEING OF STABLED HORSES

Temperature Our nineteenth-century writer Miles advocated a range between 50 and 65°F. However, many modern stables are incapable of maintaining a minimum requirement of 50° in winter conditions, most important when horses are ill. Even so, effective insulation, intelligent ventilation control and a vigilant approach will help to achieve this. Insulation is also important at the upper end of the temperature range, as is a different attitude to ventilation; but it is important to remember that draughts can be damaging even in summer, so a judgement has to be made. Also, stabled horses should never be subjected to a wide variation in temperatures during the course of a day.

Dampness Damp and wet surfaces are cold, and they invariably lower the internal temperature. The answer is generally found in the building construction, and may indicate a need for insulation, or the repair of external surfaces and rain shutes.

Wet Ceilings Uninsulated roofs invariably condense vapour and drip cold water onto animals. The standard response has been to increase ventilation rather than insulate the building, and the results are not helpful in controlling disease.

Extractor fans may be useful under certain conditions such as high humidity and high temperature

Cold Floors Uninsulated floors affect internal temperatures and may be partly remedied by good bedding material, such as deep straw. However, many systems of bedding (paper, for example) do not provide adequate surface insulation, and should only be used where floors are of a good standard. Good quality, clean straw is also getting harder to find.

Bedding Materials Innovations are on-going in the development of materials that are clean, dust free, warm and hygienic. A problem with deep-litter systems is often dampness and smells from urine retention; dust is also a significant factor, and unacceptable in any attempt to keep the respiratory tract challenge free. Dust may not be disease-causing if eliminated by a naturally working healthy tract, but it complicates matters when there is infection, and is irritant and suffocating in some situations. A lung surface clogged with dust will not be able to exchange oxygen and carbon dioxide.

Where rubber padding is used on stable floors, it is important to ensure that it does not become soiled underneath (by sealing it down). Dust and fungal spores in straw cause irritation and allergy. Horses that eat bedding are likely to have performance problems.

▶ *Always use common sense when opening the top doors of stables, what you decide to do depends on weather conditions*

Hygiene Good hygiene depends on high standards of stable management. The bedding material is an essential element of this, and also its maintenance. The surface of the bed should be skipped out late at night and cleaned out as early as possible in the morning. Drainage should ideally carry urine straight from the building. The surface beneath the horse should never be damp, cold or dirty.

Hygiene is also important for fittings, tack and implements: remember that worm eggs can stick to feed and water vessels, doors and walls; infectious organisms can reside in discharges for lengthy periods wherever they fall; and bacteria and viruses are coughed straight from horse to horse. Any of these can be carried on the hands of grooms, on brushes and buckets, on sacks and barrows. Saddles and bridles can become carriers of infection via the hands of workers or from direct contamination by horses. These are all critical in the path taken by organisms in disease, and therefore in any effort to control them.

Ventilation Advice on this has to be the most ambiguous in equine management at present. Veterinary medicine sadly provides little precise direction on it for horses; although parallels are drawn from other animals such as pigs and poultry, these are not strictly comparable, as the horse is not a sedentary producer of food. If we accept that draughts are undesirable, then we must also accept that any type of cross-ventilation is risky, except perhaps in the warmest and mildest conditions. The person responsible for environment control must be

open-minded and sensitive to changes likely to occur throughout the day and night.

Open ridges inevitably make airflows, and temperatures, impossible to control in stables and barns. An answer to this is to fully partition the stalls and place a ceiling over the horses (as the French do it); this allows ventilation of the building without subjecting the individual animal to the same fluctuations or draughts as the outer building. In barns where this is not done, disease is invariably more common and more difficult to control. Ridges in single stables should always be sealed, and no vent should ever be incapable of being closed. Air outlets should go into loft spaces or ducts, as they did in times past: they should never conduct directly to the outside.

Stable doors are usually divided in Britain and Ireland. There is ongoing debate as to the best use of top doors, the answer to which has to be: use common sense, as conditions vary, and what you do must be decided according to the prevailing weather. Thus in extreme cold, the top may be closed fully or partly; at other times it might be

▲ A horse resting in a deep paper bed. Paper bedding does not provide good surface insulation and should only be used where the surface of the floor is good

FROM HISTORY

Fulke Walwyn, the celebrated National Hunt trainer of wonderful horses – such as, for example, Mill House – was known as a 'windows man' because he was constantly adjusting doors and windows to assure the comfort of his horses. Perhaps it is significant that most modern trainers who have dispensed with this wisdom have not had his successes. Tom Dreaper, trainer of Arkle – considered by many to be the greatest chaser of all time – is quoted as saying that the most crucial aspect of stable management was to keep the horse warm and dry. The most important achievement of both of these men was to be able to keep their horses healthy, fit and sound throughout their racing careers. Certainly it must be accepted that conditions have changed: racing has become more competitive, and numbers per training unit have considerably increased – but even so, few, if any, trainers now can compare with the success of these men.

▶ *Tom Dreaper said the most crucial aspect of stable management was to keep the horse warm and dry. It worked for Arkle, here, his triple Gold Cup winner*

left open. Closed doors pose no threat when there are other sources of ventilation, though they might be dangerous when there are none. Open tops are sensible when there is no alternative air inlet, but not when horses have their heads and necks exposed to rain; except, naturally, in extreme conditions.

Air exchange is not something that can be estimated by formula. It varies with the weather conditions and the outside temperature, and that is why there is need for constant watchfulness (a vent left open on a warm day might need to be closed when it is cold). Adjustments are made according to the prevailing wind direction and strength, on ambient temperatures and on time of the day, always bearing in mind that things might change during the night. If this is not done, horses may be subjected to conditions they might be better off facing in the field. Air exchange does not need to create discomfort, since foul air can escape through a ceiling duct and fresh air can enter in plenty over a half door.

Animals with chronic disease should be catered for according to their individual needs.

International Comparison Contemporary French stabling, as well as older British yards, suggests a belief in air entry from the front of the stable only, and this seems perfectly sensible. Additional ventilation would only be used in extremely warm and windless conditions. There is generally no back wall window or vent in French racing yards, just a small outlet in the ceiling to allow foul air to escape via a lofted area above; there is no direct communication with the outside. Ceilings are at a standard height

◀ *Fixed roof lights are vital in some buildings. The ball in the centre is to discourage box-walking. Windows and fittings should be kept clean and easily adjustable. The mesh grille is a safety precaution*

The American barn system with front grills and open roof space

(98–118in/ 250–300cm), and the stable dimensions are standard (about 138–157in/ 350–400cm square), roomy and with no cross-vents, and no communicating openings at the feed troughs or in the walls.

Stable Size Inevitably there will be room for variation in the figures given above, but the horse needs a well-constructed and adequately roomy stable so that he can move about easily; and so retain the heat generated by his body in order to stay warm and infection free.

Barns American-style barns came about as a result of tightening economic factors as well as for reasons of convenience, and so that grooms and carers could work in an environment sheltered from the worst of outdoor conditions. For horses, living in such an enclosed community is not always a good idea. Infected, coughing horses will saturate the atmosphere with organisms, so none of the others will escape contact; a horse with strangles, for example, will discharge infectious material onto floors, walls and doors, spreading the disease everywhere. Allergic horses which are best kept in a dust-free atmosphere are inevitably affected by the way other horses are kept. If the barn is too cold, or draughty, all animals feel it.

IMPORTANT POINTS

- It is more difficult to treat infections in horses kept in barns.
- It is accepted that there is a critical link between prevailing conditions and recovery from infection in foals: very young foals often need incubator-like conditions when they are suffering from acute infection.
- While the mature horse does not have the same need, there is a correlation between recovery and stabling conditions.
- Highly virulent organisms will infect virtually any animal they invade, except those that have immunity; they least affect animals whose resistance is protected through understanding and good management.

STABLING STANDARDS

1   **Modern thinking** on stabling takes a different view from that of our ancestors, but there is no scientific evidence to support this.

2   **Our ancestors** benefited from generations of dependence on, and close living with, the horse; we should only discard their opinions on the basis of positive research.

3   **Except** for horses with chronic respiratory problems, standards of warmth and the provision of air exchange are basic and simply understood; the degree of current infection in intensive production strongly suggests we are getting things wrong.

4   **Horses are best kept** in individual stables with no cross-communicating divisions, peep-holes or vents.

5   **The range of temperatures** suggested by Miles (50–65°F/10–18°C) is consistent with optimum standards of disease resistance in individual horses.

6   **The elimination** of draughts is imperative.

7   **Proper insulation** is necessary, especially where the horse stands and lies, and particularly for horses in intensive training; also the elimination of damp on walls, floors and ceilings.

8   **The same standards** apply to barns and are best applied by the separation of indivdual boxes and the provision of ceilings at box level as frequently seen in France.

9   **The highest standards** of cleanliness and hygiene are needed.

10 **The level of ventilation** necessary depends on external weather conditions, ambient temperatures, and individual building characteristics (doors, windows, ceiling height, stall size, ventilation systems incorporated, the use of lights).

11 **Consider** that disease is less likely in good stabling conditions than in bad, and also less likely than in adverse outdoor conditions.

10 Allergens

Air pollution is a chronic problem that may affect horses in the field – although it must be said, it hardly bears comparison with those people who have to cope with the polluted atmosphere prevalent in cities and areas of dense population. Allergies are generally a product of domestication, though not exclusively so.

An allergy is the body's reaction to contact with a foreign substance (an allergen) such as a fungal spore: initially the body will familiarise itself with the allergen and prepare its defences against any further intrusion; subsequent exposure will cause a clinical reaction, this after a certain interval of time, perhaps days. Thus the potential for a reaction is set up by the first encounter; the illness occurs when the sufferer and the substance meet again. This may keep happening throughout life unless the sufferer develops an immunity, or treatment brings about a resolution of the problem. In many cases, as in human asthma, the condition has to be lived with, and the symptoms met with treatment as soon as they arise.

Horses generally do not suffer the acute respiratory distress seen in bad asthma cases – though it can be very serious and must never be ignored. We do not, however, expect horses to die in attacks, though the potential exists. They are also fortunate in that turning them out in a field will often reduce the symptoms and allow a return to a more normal existence, and treatments exist that are generally helpful. Many horses with a history of chronic lung disease of this nature can still manage to live a useful and fulfilling existence.

Though it would be wrong to suggest that a horse in the wild was incapable of suffering from allergies, the very nature of indoor management increases exposure to potential causes. The common allergic conditions, and their most usual clinical expression, COPD (chronic obstructive pulmonary disease), are nearly always the result of repeated low-level exposure, rather than sudden high doses of allergen. Inevitably the extent to which a horse is affected is dictated by the degree of exposure. The most common source of allergens

CAUSES OF RESPIRATORY ALLERGIES
- Bacterial and fungal spores.
- Pollens.
- Dust.
- Potentially any foreign protein.
- Hay and straw are the most common sources.
- Contamination may exist on stable surfaces.
- Dusty bedding acts as an irritant.

CONDITIONS FOR HORSES WITH COPD
- Avoid contaminated hay or dusty feeds.
- The atmosphere must be dust free.
- Bedding material must be clean of allergens and dust.
- Keep the horse in a separate stable, away from allergen sources.
- Ensure adequate air circulation but avoid draughts.
- Alternatively, ride the horse from the field and supplement grass, if needed, with dust-free feeds.

Baled hay being transported by horse and cart in Russia. Any hay that appears to be clean might still be laden with allergens

has generally been in poorly saved hay or straw, and as might be expected, these are most often found after bad harvesting conditions. Their critical assessment is therefore vital, and hay or straw that is dusty and contaminated with organisms is best given to animals other than horses. Where there is doubt, these can be analysed, though it should be possible to tell from appearance and smell. Many horse owners, however, are not good judges, particularly if they have saved the hay or straw themselves; but it should also be appreciated that clean-looking, sweet-smelling hay may often be laden with allergens and therefore unfit to be fed to horses; the same applies to straw, and whether or not to use it as bedding.

Even healthy horses react to materials that are highly contaminated, and they do not need to be COPD sufferers to choke on them. It is therefore important in trying to achieve a clean management standard that the risk of allergy be kept to a minimum. That purpose also requires physical cleanliness and hygiene within a building: there should be no growth of fungi, yeasts and/or moulds on surfaces accessible to horses; these commonly occur on damp patches, on windows and window-frames where there is regular condensation. However, it is the spores in hay and straw that cause most problems. Fungi are light enough to be blown into the air, so when horses pull at their hay, or kick up affected straw, the spores can invade the atmosphere. The same applies when beds are being laid down, straw is being shaken out, or hay is being placed in nets or racks.

STABLING FOR HORSES WITH RESPIRATORY ALLERGIES

The primary aim is to keep the horse away from anything to which it is sensitive. Instead of straw bedding, something like paper may be used, or rubber matting, though matting is usually covered with bedding material as it is a hard surface for a horse to lie

Allergens from muck-heaps may blow straight to susceptible stabled horses. Think carefully about where they are sited in relation to the stable block

on. Any other form of bedding would have to be non-allergenic, and it should also be free of dust. This rules out sawdust, shavings and peat, all of which have a high dust content, unless this is extracted. Even then, some materials, though said to be 'dust free', are by nature dusty, and the proof is seen as a black line of muck on the edge of the nostrils of horses as it is discharged. The fact that it gets to the nostrils does suggest that the air passages are protecting themselves efficiently, but it does not mean that the vital lung spaces are clear.

For any horse, perfect atmospheric cleanliness is as important as it is for ourselves. All in-contact surfaces should be clean – corners, crevices, fittings – and ceilings and

CASE NOTE

A small racehorse trainer complained that his horses were coughing (he stabled about twelve in an open barn). There had been a new purchase of hay and it was thought to be of high quality, fresh and clean. On superficial inspection it did look good, but when sniffed more closely there was a sweet if slightly suspect smell, and subsequent analysis proved it was badly contaminated. Within the barn, when one horse coughed, all the others joined in, indicating that the atmosphere was saturated with allergens; any agitation of the hay (they were all bedded on paper) resulted in bouts of sustained coughing. In order to solve the problem, not only had the hay to be replaced, but the building had to be cleaned out completely: the roof was vacuumed, the walls washed down, all dust and cobwebs removed, and all bedding taken out. Not until this was done did the coughing stop.

A lesson to be learned from this is that it is impossible to keep one animal free of allergens in a barn unless the same standards apply to all the others. In this case, no one horse suffered from chronic allergic problems, but they all showed a reaction to the hay, and most frequently as a result of air saturation as other horses perhaps coughed, or rolled, or kicked up their beds. It is a problem seen to a greater or lesser degree each autumn when new hay is fed. An allergy sufferer is best kept in a single stable, because its tolerance may be minimal, and the special conditions it needs are more difficult to attain when it is in an atmosphere shared with other horses.

roof undersurfaces should be dust free. As affected horses are generally restricted in their breathing, they should not be kept near any outside source of allergen, either: thus hay, straw or dusty material should not be left outside their stables, and they are best off not facing a muck-heap, stack or shed in which either hay or straw are kept. They must also have plenty of fresh air – although it might be said that enough is all they require, their health will still be impaired if their stable is rank and unclean, or if there is not enough air circulation. Compared to a normal horse, they may be at a disadvantage in still conditions, since these can exaggerate the symptoms and perhaps create a crisis because of the increased breathing effort and the distress that accompanies it.

Their hay, if hay is fed, must be free of spores or dust; common practice is to damp it to prevent the inhalation of allergens. Alternatively hay is replaced by good quality silage – although this can also be contaminated, especially if the bag containing it is pierced; grass is the real alternative. Anything else in the diet must be equally clean, as the future usefulness of the horse will depend on it. If control is effective, the horse can normally be used for hunting, jumping, hacking and general riding, even without drugs; competition may even be possible. But it is all a matter of degree, and the ultimate measure of success will depend on the effort made by the person managing the horse; it will also depend on the capacity of its lungs to respond to exercise.

Horses can be allergic to a host of other allergens. Pollens are particularly troublesome, as it is difficult to prevent contact at times of the year when they are plentiful.

THE CLINICAL EFFECT

Inhaled allergens cause irritation of the airways, resulting in the closure of the small channels in the lungs known as alveoli; the result is actual loss or significant reduction of the available air space. This is mostly reversible, although there are times when it is not, and then the lungs are limited in their vital capacity to exchange gases, especially when the demand increases in exercise. The effect may be only marginally imposing on a sedentary horse, but as the pace increases, so there is a call for more areas in the lungs to open and so meet the greater demand for oxygen. When a horse is flat out, especially when competing in a race, the whole of the lung capacity needs to be available so that it can express its full natural potential; without it, there are performance-limiting problems. The consequence may be that the horse simply gives in and pulls up; it may carry on at a lower speed; or it may suffer severe respiratory distress. It may also bleed into its lungs, thus further compounding the problem; this is a scenario similar to that seen in low-grade infection.

The effect is least serious for horses that are not racing; even eventers do not have the same oxygen demand in competition, and can frequently perform to the satisfaction of their rider while suffering mild respiratory impediments that a racehorse would not get away with.

Lung tissue can also be affected by environmental pollutants, though this is less common. It might happen from noxious fumes, or from emissions with an irritant effect to them, or it could happen if there was a fire.

CASE NOTE

Two broodmares within a few miles of each other were badly allergic, with marked breathing difficulties. One suffered when kept indoors and exposed to hay or straw of almost any quality; she was not helped by drugs. When turned out, however, she quickly returned to normal, only suffering when she was kept in (mostly during the winter months). She was able to have a normal breeding career. The other mare was allergic to pollen and acutely affected when counts were high. She, too, would not respond to drugs, and was badly distressed when the sun was high and the grass deep. She eventually had to be put down to prevent her suffering.

Oilseed Rape It has been said that pollen from oilseed rape causes irritation of the tract, and that this leads to prolonged bouts of respiratory disease. However, this is not an easy premise to accept, because even if the pollen were to affect a whole yard of horses, their adverse reaction should end when the pollen ceased to be shed. Moreover, if it did have that type of clinical effect, it should also affect most, if not all the horses that lived in areas where it was grown, and this is generally not the case. A far more likely explanation is that horses appearing to be affected are, in fact, suffering from infection (or some other limiting factor), and that oilseed is mistakenly blamed. It is unusual, anyway, for a pollen allergy to affect more than the odd individual animal. The idea that a whole yard would be affected would be against normal patterns for such a disease.

Oilseed rape, like many modern cereals, suffers from the double imposition of weeds and disease, and needs regular treatment with sprays to control them. Depending on the closeness of the horse to the source, it is not impossible that these could be inhaled, or where they might leach into water, ingested and so affect health.

Skin Allergies These may come from the use of systemic drugs, or insecticides, and also from insect bites, mange mites and the like. Sweet itch is thought to be due to an allergy to the saliva of biting insects, and the reaction can be very severe for some animals. Lesions are generally confined to the mane and tail, but similarly, bites of other flies may cause weals on the body and are frequently found on the back and withers,

The familiar yellow carpet of oilseed rape

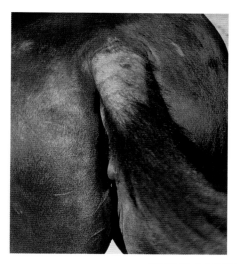

where they can lead to hard nodules that may cause problems under the saddle.

With skin allergies, the pathological processes are the same, the only difference being that the reaction is localised and there is no discernible systemic effect. However, the response to irritation can be severe, and mutilation from scratching occurs. Some cases are raw and debilitating, and efforts to control the problem include such extreme measures as using horse-clothing the flies cannot penetrate, or stabling the horse at times when they are on the wing. Drugs, by and large, are not effective in dealing with problems of the nature of sweet itch, which does not

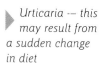 *Horse with sweet itch lesion on tail*

Urticaria -- this may result from a sudden change in diet

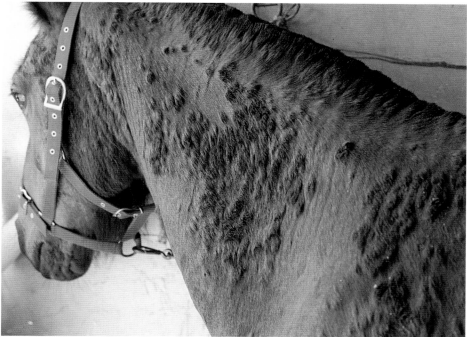

occur in areas devoid of the particular fly; it only occurs in months when the fly is about. Some animals grow out of the condition, while others are simply kept in a state of reduced misery with drug treatment.

Bleeding Maximal demand for air in already compromised lung tissues is the most probable cause of bleeding into the lungs – or 'exercise-induced pulmonary haemorrhage' (EIPH) – and inevitably this condition impedes a horse already gasping for breath. The root cause could be dust, dirt or anything else, including infection and allergy, that limits available lung space.

From a clinical standpoint, virtually all horses that bleed will already have detectable lung damage, most likely due to (often undiagnosed) chronic infection, or chronic allergy. The incidence of bleeding appears to have increased substantially in recent times, and this parallels the previously mentioned apparent rise of infection (that has, presumably, precipitated it). There are all sorts of theories relating to cause, and equally diverse suggestions relating to remedy.

In work carried out by British scientists, rubber horseshoes and uphill courses are mentioned as a means of reducing bleeding. It had been hypothesised that the cause was concussion, and that the rubber shoes would lessen the impact; also that uphill courses would relieve pressure from the lungs by moving the centre of gravity backwards. This seems to be in clear contradiction of clinical reality, and to ignore the part played by previous pathology in causing the problem. It is also extremely unlikely that either rubber shoes or uphill courses will alter the incidence, especially as the demand on the lungs when working uphill is greatly increased and would be exaggerated at racing pace.

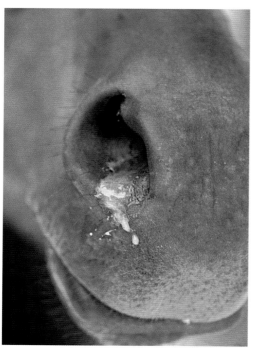

For many years Lasix, a diuretic, has been used with some effect to reduce clinical bouts of bleeding, especially in the USA where it is a permitted drug in some racing states; the theory is that lowering the blood pressure by using Lasix is beneficial. If this is correct, the idea that concussion plays a part in the condition is even harder to equate.

Bleeding occurs in the upper part of the lungs, and this is a universal finding. In horses that are chronic bleeders there is nearly always a detectable impediment to breathing, particularly noticeable at rest: the depth and rate are abnormal, and the lungs do not empty fully; neither are they capable of filling fully. After work, abnormal lung sounds are heard (wheezes and dead areas) and the post-work breathing rate is increased.

The fact that bleeding occurs from the upper parts of the lung is not that difficult to explain. Most low-grade infec-

Horse with mucopurulent nasal discharge indicating respiratory disease

tions occur and are detected in the dependent parts, meaning that the areas through which the normal breathing at rest is conducted are the most likely to become clogged up and dysfunctional. When the horse is working there is a demand for more functional lung space, a demand which will be affected by the stiffness of the conditions – the ground, any incline, and if the horse is jumping: the nostrils are flared and the upper air passages adapted to facilitate maximal air intake; this occurs when all the limbs are off the ground. Towards the end of a gallop, the horse may be gasping for air, and because the lungs are not in a condition to satisfy demands, bleeding most probably results; and it might be suggested that this happens in the healthier areas because they are being asked to over-expand to make up for those areas that are closed off.

Bleeding does not seem to occur (or is less common) in young horses that have never had a breathing impediment. The incidence of bleeding very clearly increases after clinical episodes of respiratory disease in a yard.

HOW TO COPE WITH ALLERGENS

1   **An allergy** is a clinical condition that needs proper understanding and diagnosis, best provided by a vet.

2   **Allergies** can affect any type of horse and are the most common cause of respiratory problems in riding horses (other than racehorses and competition horses, where the greatest problems arise from infection).

3   **Allergies** are most commonly associated with the types of spores and fungi found in hay and straw and that may grow on walls, windows and fixtures. They can also be caused by pollens, so affecting the horse outdoors, which may have to be stabled at times of risk.

4   **It is vital** to be scrupulous in dealing with sources; hay should be tested for freedom from dust and allergens, and straw is best avoided.

5   **Keep stables** for affected horses spotlessly clean; remove dust, dirt and cobwebs from doors, walls and ceilings.

6   **Free access to air** is imperative for any horse suffering from advanced respiratory disease.

7   **Contact allergies** can be caused through sprayed wood shavings and treated timbers, for example.

8   **The most obvious** means of dealing with an allergy is by avoiding exposure, and, where this is understood, drug use may be minimised.

9   **There are good clinical** treatments for acute attacks and drugs are available for inhalation, or oral consumption, to relieve symptoms; ask your vet.

10   **Bleeding** from the lungs during exercise may be a consequence of any form of lung disease, so affected animals are best dealt with by treating them as allergy sufferers and eliminating dust and any sources of contamination; they must also be kept warm to help avoid infection.

11 Breeding

The horse is not the most naturally fertile of the domesticated animals. The chart illustrates an interesting statistic which comes from the published returns of the British, Australian and New Zealand Thoroughbred authorities.

IN BRITAIN AND IRELAND
In 1971 of 14,555 mares registered, 7,486 live foals were produced (or 51 per cent)
In 1996, of 22,266 mares, 11,304 live foals were produced (or 51 per cent)

IN AUSTRALIA
In 1971 of 18,177 mares, 6,848 foals were produced (37.6 per cent)
In 1996 of 32,042 mares, 17,957 foals were produced (56 per cent)

IN NEW ZEALAND
In 1971 of 5,258 mares, 3,108 foals were produced (59.1 per cent)
In 1996 of 7,443 mares, 4,372 foals were produced (58.7 per cent)

While the figures do not advertise the success of modern veterinary technology (the 1971 Australian figures were unusually low), some of the total of British and Irish mares will not have been covered; Australian figures include non-stud-book mares; and the New Zealand figures apply only to stallions covering ten or more mares. The conception rates based on confirmed pregnancies for British and Irish mares will be higher, but the overall picture across the range shows the nature of equine breeding. There was a percentage improvement in some of the interim figures, but this has not been sustained. An important point is that we do not know to what extent variations are influenced by environmental factors and to what they show a failure of management to influence the situation. It must also be considered that economic problems could play a part when mares are not covered.

THE CONCEPTION PROCESS

Fertility The gestation period of the mare is eleven months, and a very large foal will inevitably cause wear and tear to the equine uterus; as a result, mares often have barren years. Also, not infrequently, Nature's way is to protect them from excessive use, whereby a type of contraceptive mechanism is activated as long as the foal is suckling; thus a significant percentage will not come into season while they have a foal at foot. Inevitably this is of great benefit to the foal, since the dam is better able to watch and protect her offspring, and better able to feed it.

The mare's relatively long oestrus period (four to seven days) also means that infertility is more likely, for two main reasons. First, for conception to occur, mares should be covered within twenty-four hours of ovulation – and preferably before it, as many mares start to reject the stallion as soon as the follicle has been shed. That is not to say that post-ovulation mating is destined to be infertile, though the chance that it will be increases with every hour that passes. Conception depends on the fertility of the stallion as well as the mare, and is particularly affected by the longevity of his semen, which may be measured in days for some, hours for others; a fertile mating thus means

The natural way: a stallion approaches a mare in a herd in Argentina

covering as near in time as possible to ovulation. On studs where management and veterinary controls are at their most efficient, mating will nearly always meet this criterion. Secondly, the length of oestrus means the uterine tract is unduly open to external influences, and foreign matter, including organisms, may enter through it. Thoroughbreds in particular seem prone to vaginal windsucking, and this can irritate the lining tissues and lay the area open to infection.

FACTORS AFFECTING MARE FERTILITY

- Season, temperature, daylight time, grass.
- Inadequate hormonal stimulation.
- Infection, including venereal diseases and from vaginal windsucking.
- Poor uterine involution.
- Health and nutrition.

The Grass Stallion Where a stallion is allowed to run with his mares, he will manage the whole process with a degree of design and control that suggests instinct, hormones and genetic influence. He will keep his mares banded together, and controls their movements; he will not allow them to wander at will, and he does not welcome human interference. As a mare comes in season she will be covered no more times than is necessary to get her in foal, and instinct tells him when this is likely to be most effective; thus he does not cover repeatedly, and so his energies should be optimally effective. Of course, a mare that stays on for a long period may spoil this scheme, especially if the signals she puts out are misleading.

STUD MANAGEMENT PRACTICES

Today's stud management tends to exercise maximum control over the whole process of reproduction. Teaser stallions and vets are employed to establish the stage of a mare's cycle and determine the optimum time to cover. In Thoroughbred breeding, mares are seldom turned out with a stallion, and a mare is restrained during covering with twitches, hobbles and kick-defying boots; if the stud manager is lucky, she will conceive with only one covering, meaning that more mares can be taken to the stallion. For the mare, as might be imagined, there is no love or pleasure; the whole process is thoroughly clinical and contrived, and any pleasure on her part has to be in the confinement, the labour and the offspring.

The reality of course, as the recorded figures show, is that modern practices have not significantly affected the course of Nature. With ever-increasing numbers of mares, and ever-developing technology, live foal returns only demonstrate that mare fertility is as poor as it always has been. As statistics suggest a variable picture, there is occasion to ask that if modern medicine cannot alter this either up or down, then what can? And to what extent might environmental factors be implicated?

Veterinary Services The development of equine fertility control began with internal manipulation. An experienced vet could tell if the tract was clinically normal and when the mare was going to ovulate. These matters are vital to the Thoroughbred stud, as artificial insemination is not permitted, and conserving the use of the stallion is economically essential.

Developments in laboratory procedures went hand-in-hand with better clinical understanding of infection and other diseases of the reproductive tract; moreover the ultrasonic scanner is purported to make diagnosis simpler. Also, the widening breeding scene has meant more veterinary involvement, and the opportunity for more controlled research and innovation; nowadays embryo transfer is yet another option, although this has yet to prove itself economically viable.

The ultrasound scanner is probably the most significant innovation in modern stud management; it has made objective examination of the tract a more defined procedure, and it has allowed for more precise pregnancy diagnosis and for monitoring the development of the foetus in a manner similar to human medicine. However, the importance of foal development is not to be compared with that of the human baby: there are not the same disease conditions, nor are there the same priorities regarding what should be done when abnormality is found. Generally, a mare either carries her foal or she does not; if it turns out to be abnormal, simple decisions have to be made, and these are mostly economic in nature.

Ultimately, however, it has to be accepted that on the basis of international returns, all these modern developments have done nothing to improve live foal numbers. Veterinary medicine needs to justify the expense and the intrusion, as the only figure that can be said to have been significantly improved is that relating to twins. As these

FACTORS AFFECTING STALLION FERTILITY

- Lack of libido.
- Abnormal sperm, including short viability.
- Venereal infection.
- Physical abnormalities of reproductive organs.
- Inability to cover.
- Health and nutrition.

are mostly non-viable and very seldom an economic proposition if they do survive because they are generally so small and weak, they are bad news to the mare owner and their arrival creates bad publicity for the stud. Rossdale in his book *The Horse from Conception to Maturity*, states that the incidence of twins conceived in Great Britain and Ireland is about 1 per cent of all pregnancies. According to the 1997 Statistical Analysis, 30 mares produced twins from a total of 22,413 mares registered. Mares that aborted, slipped or produced dead foals numbered 1,543 in the same year, some of which could well also have carried undiagnosed twins. It does not make impressive reading from a veterinary viewpoint.

Covering under human supervision is unnatural and not always without risk

Management Priorities The stallion owner has always wanted to cover as many mares as possible with each stallion: this is what decides the economic success of the business enterprise. It is achieved by limiting the number of coverings, so that for the stud, the most significant statistic is the number per verified conception; and as long as fertility is high, the number will be low. The mare goes home in foal, and depending on the conditions of the contract, the stud is likely to be paid. Twins, hopefully, are eliminated. The lower the number of coverings and the higher the number of mares in foal, the more successful is the stud, providing it has commercial stallions and attracts plenty of mares.

All this becomes increasingly difficult to achieve in years when natural patterns change. The colder the spring, the longer mares take to come into season naturally, and if there is a grass shortage at the time when fertility should be at its highest (due to warmth, daylight and growing conditions), the mare's cycle might not take place at all: she might not come into season, or produce fertile follicles, or ovulate; infection is also more common in these conditions, and so of course conception rates will be down.

The Mare In order to breed a foal, the ideal is to use a young mare with a viable follicle and a uterus free from stress and infection: for her, conception rates will be high, as will live foal percentages.

Some mares stay in season for periods ranging from days to weeks, particularly in the early parts of the year when light is limited, grass is scarce and she has not settled into a cycling pattern. On examination, it will be found that the ovaries are inactive and there is no viable follicle, in which case covering the mare is usually wasteful, and may even help to introduce infection. Furthermore, drugs will have no appreciable effect; even if it is possible to precipitate ovulation, she will probably fail to conceive.

The mare's natural approach to the breeding season is to welcome it slowly. Her body attunes itself as the days lengthen and the months warm up, to times when grass is in its full lush growth. The purpose of this is to dictate the time her foal will be born: she wants it to be met with warm days and plenty for her to feed it on. The reasons that we try to change this are all commercial: breeders want earlier foals that will look bigger and more 'forward' in the sale ring; studs want a longer covering season.

FOALING

Although mares have no voluntary control over when they actually conceive, obviously if the foal arrives when there is grass and warmth it will be to its best advantage. And so it is interesting that the mare does seem able to exercise real control as to when she actually gives birth: to a limited extent, it appears she can delay her delivery time to suit her circumstances, as most observed mares foal at night, and many closely watched mares foal as soon as they are left unattended. This is remarkable, but can be explained by considering life in the wild, where no mare would want to foal when there was any sort of risk, particularly the threat of a possible enemy when she was at her most vulnerable. Darkness offers some protection, and if she foals early in the night, the foal has time to get to its feet and suck (often achieved within minutes) before break of day when the risk of being detected by predators is much higher. Thus far instinct, over millions of years, has helped her; besides which she usually foals in a very short time, the whole process having evolved to minimise danger and enable her and her foal to make a quick escape if necessary.

When a mare foals in a field of other mares, all the raw aggression of her nature will come to the fore if anything or anyone challenges her foal. Filled with maternal concern, she will parade and fight violently to keep the inquisitive and the aspiring surrogate away; rescuing mother and offspring is not a task for the faint-hearted. However, it has to be assumed the other mares are only showing a mixture of curiosity and protection, even if the new mother fails to appreciate that.

Foaling is a potentially explosive event, making human attendance of valuable stock an absolute necessity. Some mares foal with great violence and complete disregard for their own well-being, almost as if the foal is a foreign body they have to expel. In the process they may rupture the tissues of the vagina, vulva and rectum, perhaps so badly that it is doubtful whether they will ever have another pregnancy – and if they do, the same mares tend to damage themselves again; it is in their nature. But as soon as the foal is born, they show it all possible love and attention.

When foaling in the open the foal must get to its feet quickly and find the teat. The mare is attempting to guide the foal to her milk

Other mares seem to lack stimulus and take time to foal, especially in the early months of the year when extended gestation periods and low levels of hormonal stimulation seem to be more common.

All these troubles come from trying to move the mare away from her natural cycle.

Foal Rejection Although there are no statistics to support the view, it would seem that the problem of foal rejection is increasing. This is a condition seen in both Thoroughbreds and Arabs, and it is mystifying because it is against every natural instinct the mare possesses. In many cases it can be attributed to pain relating to foaling: young mares that produce relatively large foals can bruise themselves severely; their udders are sore and swollen, and when the foal sucks it is painful; also, the hormones that stimulate milk let-down cause uterine resolution, bringing more pain. The mare kicks out and frightens the foal, and she may even try to kill it – and in many cases there is no reversing this tendency.

Fostering When a mare dies in foaling or while suckling a foal, the foal is reared by hand, or is fostered when a foster mare is available. The more highly bred a mare, the less likely she is to take to fostering, although in some large studs, a band of more

CASE NOTE

It was thought that the mare Albigold was the last mare to be put in foal to the Classic winning stallion, Ragusa. Alas, she produced live and healthy twins: a small but well formed filly and a bigger colt. It was decided that from a commercial viewpoint, the filly would have a certain value, were it possible to rear her: even if she stayed small, it was a very good racing line, and with good management, mares that were born twins could be helped to produce single foals. Thus it was hoped to redeem something from what otherwise looked to be a total loss, as the colt would never have the size to be of value (as it proved); and even if he did, who would want to breed from a stallion born a twin?

Unfortunately the problems were exacerbated when the mare decided she couldn't handle two foals and wanted to be rid of the filly (she adored her colt). Despite every effort to change her mind, she became increasingly violent and showed she was quite prepared to kill it, finally making it necessary to find a foster mare. Within twelve hours, a big

Thoroughbred mare, aptly called Broken Union (herself a very successful National Hunt dam), was brought to the yard, laden with milk. She took to the filly without grunt or hesitance, and it guzzled itself sick on all there was to have – literally, because the next day it was scouring, and developed acute colic. Very sadly, and despite all sorts of efforts to save it, the foal died.

commonly bred mares is kept solely for fostering purposes, usually ponies or light draught mares, docile and amenable. When a mare's services are called for, her own foal is quickly taken away. Invariably she accepts the new foal, though to begin with it can be a very trying process. Sedatives and twitches may have to be used; ointment may have to be smeared on her nostrils to stifle her sense of smell; and where a foster mare has lost her own foal, it might be skinned and the skin draped over the fostered foal.

Sometimes mares will not conceive when they have a foal at foot. If they are valuable and it is determined that they should go straight back in foal, their own foal may be taken from them (after it has had colostrum and become adjusted to life outside the womb) and fostered. There is then a greater chance the mare will go back in foal without missing a year.

THE BREEDING CYCLE

The Foaling Heat The newly foaled mare comes in season again usually seven to ten days after giving birth. In young, healthy mares it is a short and fertile oestrus, although the level of fertility is dependent on the degree to which her uterus has returned to normal after eleven months of being stretched. She will probably only accept the stallion for, perhaps, twenty-four hours or so; though if everything is in order, she will be pregnant again. However, if she retained her afterbirth when the foal was born, the chances of conception will be reduced because she could well be harbouring infection which will take time to clear up.

If she does not go in foal on this heat, she will come in season again about three weeks later, and from then on will assume a normal pattern of coming in season about every three weeks and staying on for four to seven days, until she conceives again.

Barren and maiden mares start their breeding year by displaying the outward signs of a slowly awakening reproductive system. While there are always exceptions, the natural process is attuned to the progressing year, to the emergence of leaves and flower buds, to singing birds and glorious sunshine. Many studs attempt to cut short the process by bringing mares indoors in winter and lengthening the days artificially with lights and feeding them concentrates. Every other day they are introduced to a teaser; they see other mares come on, go off, and be turned out – and invariably by July they will nearly all have obliged.

A mare that does not go in foal continues cycling, though as the season progresses, the length of time that she is receptive shortens to perhaps four days: this period is marked first by a low-grade heat, then over two days her cycle gradually builds to ovulation, then there is a rapid 'cooling down' period. The barren mare has various disease or mechanical problems which man and Nature generally attempt to reverse in order that she can continue to breed; all sorts of artificial stimuli may be introduced to control the cycle and ultimately increase fertility. However, Nature's hand has always been the ultimate measure of this, and based on live foal percentages, there is not much sign that we are able to out-think her.

Returning to the 1997 Statistical Analysis, from a total of 22,413 mares at stud in Great Britain and Ireland, 4,013 were not covered and 334 were covered by unregistered stallions; these figures can be taken to be fairly typical for any year. Of 18,066 mares thus covered by registered stallions, 11,301 produced live foals (including the thirty that had twins); 1,543 either aborted, slipped or died (639); and there were 1,868 barren mares (10.3 per cent), 3,794 (21 per cent) with no returns, and 894 that were otherwise discounted (exported, for example). 12,844 were considered to have conceived, giving a 73.3 per cent conception rate overall of mares covered, with a 1998 live foal percentage of 55 per cent.

Various factors would influence the number of mares not covered, not the least being that of economics; however, this figure would vary and, it needs to be suggested, economics would not be a consistent element over a wide time spell. Thus other unseen influences, such as environmental factors, need to be taken into account when considering fluctuating trends in live foal numbers.

Abortion A figure of 904 mares that slipped or aborted represents those that were tested in foal and subsequently either resorbed or were seen to lose a foal. This is 4 per cent of the total mares, or 7 per cent of those that conceived. When 1,533 mares either died or were discounted, that would add another 107 mares to this group (using the same percentages), or bringing the figure closer to 8 per cent. This fits well with the generally recognised assumption that between 10–15 per cent of mares lose foals after conception.

The Stallion Although modern influences (including injected hormones) may have intruded on Nature, fertility in the stallion, it can be said, is greater than in the mare, as most stallions can be expected to produce fertile semen. However, there are those that do not, and others whose semen only remains viable for a short period of time; and there may also be stallions lacking in libido and not wishing to cover large numbers of mares – in fact, some may not want to cover any at all.

In the wild, infertile stallions or stallions of low fertility would inevitably have a limiting influence on reproduction, although it is most likely they would only eliminate their own line as others moved in to take over. In domestication, the problem is very likely to be of significant economic importance, and furthermore poses problems of a different nature. On the one hand, the fertile and eager stallion may be asked to cover far more mares than he would consider in the wild. If management is effective, he will only cover each mare once for each foal conceived, though such ideals are seldom achieved. The uninterested stallion, on the other hand, poses great problems for his handlers, especially where artificial insemination is not allowed, and he may prove to be a total commercial loss.

Nowadays it is common for willing stallions to cover 100 mares, and some have doubled this, and more; compare this to only a matter of years ago, when a stallion's

Icelandic stallions fighting: the winner will drive the other away from the herd

book was in the region of forty mares. Taking a figure of 100, this would mean 100 coverings for 100 conceptions as a perfect outcome, and if these were evenly spread out, it would mean one covering per day for 100 days. But it is never evenly spread, and 200 coverings per mare – two per conception – would be more in line with reality, thereby doubling the workload. With 200 mares, this would mean 400 coverings, and so on. As the first two to three months of the year (before the appearance of any grass growth) are not natural breeding months, only a small percentage of mares are likely to come in season and be successfully covered. This means the bulk of the stallions' work is concentrated into the following quarter, when large numbers of mares may come on at the same time. No wonder that some decide enough is enough and refuse to play along!

This workload is stretched further with the modern practice of using some stallions in both Northern and Southern Hemispheres in the same year, thereby potentially doubling the number of mares they can cover. But it is not Nature's design, and the loss of stallions like Suave Dancer recently –as well as several others over the years – must stand as an abiding questionmark over the whole procedure.

Natural Trends The process of breeding is distilled by Nature, and follows paths and biological rhythms that all have their own reasoning. Thus the peak of natural fertility concurs with a foaling date that will bring optimum conditions for the foal. While man struggles to thwart this, it is noticeable that there are periods when everything seems to happen beyond human control – when Nature takes hold, mares go in foal without difficulty. Thus in the early spring months the vet, under constant pressure from management, struggles to find fertile follicles and spends a great deal of time swabbing, treating infection, and trying to promote oestrus, often with frustratingly poor success. Then as if by magic, big, ripe follicles grow: under the stimulus of evidently stronger internal working, there is a surge of fertility and mares go in foal. Pregnant uteri are palpated and scanned at a rate that almost leads the operator to believe that the boom has been engineered by man – but this is not so, and the truth is that the stimulus has come from Nature – and those who think otherwise will soon find out the hard way that manipulating her is never quite that easy.

Organic Standards for Mares Bad weather and environmental influences will impede a successful breeding programme: a long, cold spring limits grass production – an essential source of hormones – and will deny the mare the stimulus of light and warmth that she needs to produce ripe follicles. The reproductive tract also misses the influence of the natural oestrogens needed to cleanse it, and so the incidence of infection rises as the ovarian cycles become weaker. Fertility inevitably suffers.

There is also a considerable possibility that pesticides and other substances will have an adverse effect on hormone balances (some, like lindane and PCBs, being chemically related), as has been proven in other animals. If so, the consequences will further reduce fertility, abortion/resorption rates will be increased, and more abnormal foals will be born.

Feeding the Mare at Stud To assist the concept of an organic standard for mares, the type of diet fed should be produced organically in its entirety: oats, good hay and a simple vitamin/mineral supplement, the grass should be without artificial fertiliser, and the water as pure as nature can provide it. Her pasture should not be worm-sick or polluted with infectious organisms, and the grasses should be balanced and nutritious and not contain too high a level of succulents.

The aim is to avoid pollutants in both feed and water so as to provide the means for natural fertility; and then for the foal to be born when there is warmth and plenty of food about for its optimal development. As well as aiding fertility, lush grass generally means a more natural foaling, with less premature milk production and more predictable timing. At this time there is also better uterine involution, less risk of infection, and quicker conception rates. The mare will have nurtured the foal within her womb to her full capacity, and the foal will have the best chance of being strong and healthy when it arrives.

CASE NOTE

Significantly reduced fertility was suspected in 1990, when there was a protracted dry period with poor grass growth in April and May in Great Britain, the traditional peak of the National Hunt breeding season of Northern Hemisphere mares. The effect was country wide, and many studs were affected. As can be imagined, it takes time to realise there is a problem, with each stud only seeing its own results. If mares are not going in foal, questions are asked about the stallions, the feeding is looked at, each mare is assessed, and reasons are sought for every failure.

That year it was noticeable that mares were slow to come into season, nor did they produce good follicles; also they kept coming back in heat. Stallions were exonerated because they were producing foals (if more slowly), but the coverings per conception were high and too many mares were breaking. In retrospect, clinically the problem was related to poor grass growth, as low-grade and non-specific infections were also common and difficult to deal with. Even maiden mares were found with purulent cervical discharges, though these proved sterile on culture and responded to treatment. Eventually most mares went in foal, but they were late, and the stallions had more work than normally would have been the case – though live foal percentages for the following year at 61 per cent did not reflect the problem.

Of course, one bad year is hardly a crisis, but if this was a warning, there are many aspects of horse management that need to be looked at, especially the fields and what might grow in them. Live foal percentages have since fallen back to the middle or lower fifties, to where they were in fact before technology assumed such importance. In the USA, 41,801 foals were born in 1991, a 5.3 per cent reduction on the previous year, but this was probably an economic effect. In Australia, the live foal percentage was 52 per cent, down from 57 per cent in the previous year, though the reasons for this are not provided.

It should not be forgotten that Thoroughbred mares get more attention than any other breed: there is very precise control over every aspect of fertility, records are realistic and accurate, and results cannot be distorted.

WHAT **YOU** CAN DO	# HOW TO DEAL WITH THE PROBLEMS OF BREEDING

1 **Most stud farms** are intensively run and thus a source of risk to the organically minded breeder; an organic concept here would probably call for a home-kept stallion, which would be impractical; so it is important to minimise any risk.

2 **Mindful that disease** is an everyday occurrence on large studs, limit the duration of a mare's stay; walk-in only if allowed, and isolate returning mares as far as possible.

3 **Mares infectious for EVA** or EHV are a threat to others in-foal (both viruses are transmitted by coughing); call your vet to any coughing mare coming from stud.

4 **Mares** that have been away for a duration may need immediate worming; also, they might best be kept isolated for three weeks (maybe in an open barn), then wormed again to catch maturing larvae.

5 **Studs,** generally, are eager to limit disease, and need to be assisted in the way of swabs and tests for organisms like CEM, or vaccination for 'flu or abortion.

6 **Because mares** arriving at a stud farm will have come from many different locations, there is a danger they will bring with them a variety of organisms and infections; these can then infect animals on the stud one after another, thus causing protracted infections, which may then be transmitted to ridden horses on their return home.

7 **Stallions** with EVA may spread the virus through their semen; always enquire before sending a mare away, also about the general disease situation.

8 **The breeding cycle** should be naturally aided, not drug induced, and the mare could always be pregnancy tested at home, thus reducing time spent at stud.

9 **Foals suffer** any adult infections like those mentioned, but also get, and can die from, infectious diarrhoea, *Rhodococcus*, and heavy worm infestations; the less time they spend at stud the better for their health.

10 **Feeding** at stud is unlikely to be organic, and hay and grasses may be heavily dressed with artificial fertilisers, all factors which will have greatest significance for the foal at foot as well as the growing foetus.

12 The Development of Young

Any attempt to provide organic standards for a foal must encompass the whole period from conception onwards. Obviously this includes its development within the mare, and must therefore dictate the standards to which she is kept throughout her time at stud, and subsequent to it. To obtain optimum development it is important that the foal's diet, once it is feeding with the mare, has adequate protein, an easily digested energy source, and does not contain fibre it cannot digest (though it must have enough fibre when its gut is ready to digest it).

The quality of the pasture is critical. Worm control is essential on the basis of a drug-free regime, except where clinical disease occurs, and then the wormers used should be environmentally friendly; the rotation of grazing with other stock is important. When there is a risk of mineral deficiency, or imbalance, this should be anticipated and supplements provided before physical changes are apparent.

Development is vital on a day-to-day basis. Any physical set-back needs to be noticed quickly and the cause found, as any prolonged disease is capable of limiting the final potential of the animal.

FOAL STATISTICS

A number of interesting statistics come from USA Thoroughbred records. Using as a yardstick the 3,476 foals born in 1900, ten-year totals of foals born went down 46 per cent in the second decade of the century, then rose strongly – up 72 per cent in the twenties – but slowed to a 28 per cent increase in the forties. They went up by 84 per cent in the sixties, and the trend continued upwards until 1987, when the total was 50,917 foals born; after this there was a fall of 18 per cent in the next eight years, presumably as a result of over-supply. The 1996 total (35,400) was equivalent to 69 per cent of the 1986 (the peak year) crop; and there is no suggestion that this fall was due to anything other than market factors.

In Australia, mare numbers peaked at 44,374 in 1985, producing 19,918 foals (45 per cent); they fell back to 28,338 in 1998, producing 16,827 foals (59 per cent). This was a fall of 37 per cent in thirteen years, roughly following the USA trend.

What all this effectively shows is that, based on British figures as well, Nature holds an unseen control over live foal crops, and man's influence is dictated largely by commerce. Horses will only be bred significantly as long as there is a live market to sell them into. Despite our love affair, they remain a luxury and need to contribute in some small way to their existence, even if only by creating pipe-dreams.

THE FOAL

From the day of its arrival, the foal is challenged by its capacity to adapt to life outside the womb. If its mother has poor quality colostrum, it is unlikely to survive the range of organisms in her immediate environment; and colostrum quality might be affected by age, and also by disease and malnutrition. Moreover, if the milk that follows the colostrum is in short supply, or poor in quality, the foal will be backward and unthrifty. Without a sufficient and properly balanced supply of calcium and phosphorus, it will grow weak bone that is likely to break or become diseased. If the paddocks are too intensively stocked, it will be exposed to worm eggs and larvae to a degree that might threaten its life; if the weather is too wet, it might get pneumonia; if it is too dry, *Rhodococcus* infection (an organism inhaled from dust patches in fields, barns and contaminated stables) is more common, thought to be a disease of lowered resistance. In other words, foals that lack natural protection are most likely to be sick, and if there is too much crowding, viral diarrhoea becomes a problem.

Most studs exercise constant vigilance against infection. The very act of collecting large numbers of horses together opens the way for disease, the greatest risks being abortion and paralysis, and sickness, even sometimes death, amongst the foals.

In the first few hours foals require care and protection

A Foal's First Hours Foals are at their most vulnerable in the immediate hours after birth, and they must be completely healthy and normal if they are to survive. There are certain congenital deformities and conditions that will compromise their chances; for instance, they may have weak and crooked legs that inhibit movement, or they may have trouble finding the teat and sucking it. Some are born with a condition that affects the suck reflex; these are known as 'dummies' and 'barkers'. The stronger ones seek the teat but often fail to locate it, and are generally unable to suck if they do manage to get it in their mouths; some are too weak and uncoordinated to keep their heads extended upwards and fall tamely back; others wander about and show no interest at all. Badly affected foals stand with their heads pressed to the wall, while others simply stay recumbent. The problem may be resolved by bottle feeding, if the foal will drink, and those that do not may be fed by stomach tube; however, some are brain damaged and will not recover.

At times a newborn foal is challenged by its own mother's milk, a condition similar to that affecting human rhesus-factor babies. The foal's body reacts to substances in the milk, to the extent that its red blood cells are destroyed; jaundice is a common sequel, and the condition is often terminal unless quickly diagnosed and an alternative milk source given;

FACTORS AFFECTING FOAL MORTALITY

■ Health at birth.
■ Quality and intake of colostrum, including the time of the foal's first drink.
■ Management conditions at the time of birth: good hygiene, warmth and care are crucial.
■ Congenital and hereditary conditions.
■ Infection from bacteria, viruses and worms.

replacement transfusion may be needed. Foals that survive must not drink their dam's milk again until perhaps forty-eight hours after birth, by which time they will not be affected by the milk at all. If it is feared they have not had enough colostrum and are therefore inadequately protected from infection, their blood can be monitored and help provided through alternative means: for example, plasma can be collected from an unrelated adult horse and given intravenously.

It is well known that colostrum is vital to good health, and it is the only way that lactating mammals can provide their young with a certain immunity against the infections they will meet as soon as they are on the ground. This does not have to be some virulent disease with any obvious line of contact – organisms such as *Salmonella* can come from carrier animals (even the dam), or from contamination through others, and even less serious organisms may cause fatal disease in foals that are not protected. The critical time is the first two days, but colostrum should be drunk within the first hour after birth to be certain it is of maximum benefit. This is because after twenty-four hours the foal is generally unable to absorb the antibodies from the bowel any more; and in some cases the time gap can be shorter than this. The importance of an early drink is therefore critical, even if the first feed is to be given by bottle.

A foal is put at risk when a mare runs milk before foaling, because it will not have had the benefit of the colostrum containing the vital antibodies – however, colostrum from another mare may be given, and professional foaling units try to have a store of frozen colostrum they can use in such situations.

Another problem which may arise in the first day or two of the foal's life is failure to pass meconium, or the first dung. This is more common in colts than in fillies, and it can lead to severe abdominal pain and colic which is potentially dangerous until relieved. Rupture of the bladder also sometimes occurs (perhaps during foaling): the abdomen gradually fills with urine and none is passed in a normal manner, and surgery is needed to correct the problem.

Flexural deformities are the result of unbalanced growth between the bones and tendons; in bad cases the limbs may be very bent, or completely upright, and may require radical treatment, even surgery.

Some foals are born with a part of their bowel missing, and depending on the part involved, the outcome may or may not be terminal. On the other hand, lack of a natural anal opening is sometimes easily remedied. More common hereditary conditions are palate deformities, parrot mouth, and the propensity to laryngeal paralysis. In fact these conditions could be eliminated altogether if breeding authorities instigated a more stringent selection policy.

Weak Foals Foals that are born weak and sickly often have little chance of survival. A common cause of weakness is herpes virus infection, which usually brings death within a matter of hours. Premature foals need special care and conditions: a warm,

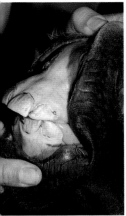
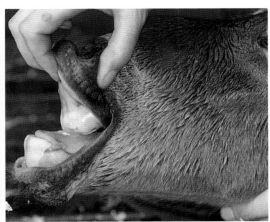
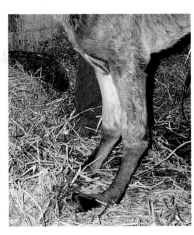

*(above left)
Parrot mouth but
some apposition of
teeth. Such horses
can expect a normal
life span*

*(centre) 'Hog' or 'sow'
mouth. There is no
apposition here and
the foal may be
unable to graze or
survive*

*(right) Poor front
limb development;
may improve with
time and help. In the
wild the foal might
not survive*

clean box, with adequate air but no draughts, help with feeding if needed, immune monitoring and constant vigilance. In particularly bad cases, the full range of veterinary intensive care procedures may be needed. Happily, in well run establishments foal mortality is not high (0–2 per cent), but the risks will increase, however, concomitant with heavy stocking and lower standards of management.

The Growing Foal

Healthy foals may be turned out to grass with their dams within days, or even hours, of birth. The best policy is to let them all run together, when there should be no risk as long as the paddocks are safely fenced, free of dangerous obstacles, and provide adequate shelter. Exercise combined with a good and plentiful milk supply is very important if development is to be normal at this critical time. Foals born with weak, and sometimes even crooked legs often strengthen up and improve in conformation; they browse alongside their dams and soon start to pick at different grasses and herbage as she eats. The mare, too, benefits in her milk production with plenty of grass.

The Development of the Digestive System The foal's digestive system is virtually sterile at birth. It is introduced to organisms from the teat of its mother, its immediate surrounds, and almost anything it touches; some of these organisms can cause serious health problems, such as worm eggs and larvae, but others are beneficial, such as those that are essential to digestion throughout life. As we have said, the newborn system is adapted to an exclusively milk diet. Lactose is its principal sugar, and this is broken down by the enzyme lactase; lactase gradually disappears, however, as the animal matures into adulthood (from three years onwards). This is why adult animals are unable to digest milk, and why they often scour when it is given to them.

This immature system is not, then, adapted to digest fibre, and although a mare's milk is lower in fat, protein and ash content than a cow's, for instance, it is higher in lactose, which is the energy source, and vital for vigour and movement. The foal starts to nibble grass within a few days, thus adding a new source of energy and protein to supplement what it gets from its dam. At this stage its large bowel is incapable of producing the vitamins which are vital as life goes on. It will pick at its mother's hay and begin to show an interest in her feed (if she is given any) but it will not gorge itself on any of these; its intake will increase gradually over the early months, and so the stomach and intestine develop and adapt to coping with herbage by degree rather than in a sudden rush. It is also important to appreciate that although the foal will eat concentrates from an early stage, this is not always in its own best interests, and those providing it must show understanding for the state of development of the digestive tract.

Dentition The appearance of a foal's different teeth is a good indication as to the stage of development of the digestive system as a whole. We have established that at birth Nature provides only for a milk diet, the digestion of which requires no teeth whatever: there is no need for gastric acid to digest it, as milk is broken down and absorbed in the small intestine, so there is no need for saliva to be produced during feeding, so there is no need for the chewing process. All the digestive processes we understand develop in their own time.

It follows from this that the introduction of concentrates at too early a stage may create digestive problems. If not properly digested they may irritate the gut lining which will result in diarrhoea and unthriftiness, and the long-term effects may be malabsorption, deficiency and stunted growth; ulcers are also a possible outcome.

By the end of the first year the foal will have grown a fully functional set of deciduous incisors capable of coping with plants and herbage; this means that the body is fully ready for forage consumption, and can therefore dispense with milk altogether. In fact, most mares are dried off long before this, and foals can be successfully weaned once they start eating solids in the early months of their lives – though exactly when to wean depends, of course, on circumstances. The death of a mare must be the most common cause of early weaning. In this case the dam's milk can be substituted with artificial milk replacers, of which there are many varieties; but it must be appreciated that it is important to follow as closely as possible the horse's natural pattern of diet and feeding habits – moreover the problems with early weaning are often more to do with adaptation and behaviour than with nutrition.

The stomach adapts gradually to the introduction of solids, as does the large bowel, and any attempt to speed up this development will cause problems. Spring grass is an ideal introduction to adult feeding patterns, and new foals will be seen picking around almost as soon as they are turned out; this is the natural way of gut development. They also pick at hay given to the mare, and soon have their heads in her feed bucket. As long as the intake is gradual and the food is suitable, the foal's digestion will adapt to the change and no harm will be done.

BABY TEETH

- At birth (or within two weeks), a foal has three cheek teeth on each jaw as well as the two central incisors.

- Two more incisors appear at about one month to six weeks.
- The laterals arrive at six months, these being fully in wear at a year.
- The first permanent molar appears at nine to twelve months;
  the second at two years;
  and the third at three-and-a-half to four years.

Coprophagia The foal's inclination to coprophagia, or eating faeces, is instinctive, because in this way it can obtain a healthy flora of organisms. However, in doing so it may also risk becoming contaminated with less desirable agents of disease – but that may be the price to be paid. Ideally the dam would have no worms or pathogenic organisms, although that is not likely to be the case where there is any form of intensive production – and in fact it is thought that a continued low-level exposure to worms eventually leads to a certain level of immunity. For many reasons this is unlikely ever to be full immunity – in any case, there is such a wide variety of parasites that immunity to worms is likely to fail in the face of a heavy challenge, or where resistance is lowered through hunger or other types of disease.

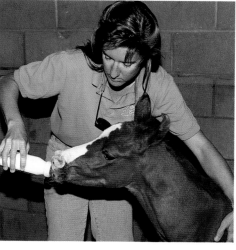

Artificially feeding foals is a gentle procedure

ARTIFICIALLY FED FOALS

The relationship between a mare and foal is no more unique than that between any animal and its offspring. However, a disruption of this relationship can have unfortunate consequences, especially in the future behaviour of the foal; this might be if a mare dies and the foal is raised by hand, when a close substitute relationship develops with a human carer. Take the following anecdote as a case in point.

A light bay gelding had been orphaned as a foal and reared by hand; he was big, playful, and full of strength and attractive movement. A handsome horse, he was four and his intended purpose was National Hunt racing. However, his owners couldn't get him to go forward and the matter was getting worse by the day. A lovely horse to deal with in the stable, he was always thinking and eager to show how bright he was, and when ridden, he gave the impression he was forward-going and willing; but after a while, he would become awkward and wilful, rearing dangerously and with clear intent. One day, working with other horses, he went at a nice canter for a circuit of a round gallop, then suddenly stopped. He let the others go half a circuit ahead, then took after them, flat out; but as soon as he passed them, he stopped dead again. In the end he was too dangerous even out hunting, and although he was as kind as a kitten at home, no one ever managed to cure him of his wayward behaviour. He appeared to have everything, but the fact that he had been brought up as a pet and had missed out on any sort of maternal bond seemed to have irreversibly affected his temperament.

TOWARDS WEANING

Growth and development are critical to the future strength and well-being of any horse, and anything that inhibits normal growth is likely to affect the quality of the finished product; this includes size, health, strength and athletic ability. Any set-back while the animal is developing may affect its future growth, especially where tissues suffer damage of a nature that will lead to problems in the future. As an example, physical damage to the bowel lining may have a residual effect on absorption and mineral balances; similarly, destruction of liver or lung tissue may leave an animal that is never able to express its full potential.

Abnormal development is reflected in body condition, skin, coat and general appearance and well-being. Enlarged growth plates are common in late summer, especially if the ground is hard, and they are particularly exaggerated in calcium deficiency; if ignored, they may lead to permanent disfigurement, or at the very least unsoundness.

Over-feeding The practice of over-feeding foals and yearlings to make them big and strong is suspected of being one of the causes of osteochondritis (OCD). It can be postulated that either the excess of bodyweight on immature bone leaves it more open to injury, or that the mineralisation of bone is affected by the diet, either through malabsorption, improper mineral balance, or deficiency.

WHAT YOU CAN DO

THINKING OF THE FOAL

1 **Make sure** your mare is kept in clean and wholesome conditions during pregnancy, fed an organic diet and given good-quality drinking water; follow these guidelines and foal development should not be affected by any adverse external influence of a toxic nature.

2 **The immediate need** after birth is a supply of quality colostrum that contains antibodies to deal with perinatal infections; colostrum quality can be tested and serum given as an alternative if deficient.

3 **Development** generally is subject to balanced intakes, free of toxic contaminants, and there must be adequate protein for growth, adequate energy, and balanced mineral and vitamin intakes.

4 **Worm control** is a concern, especially for foals that have been away at stud; ascarids are an accepted problem, though regular monitoring by dung analysis is wise in cases of high risk.

5 **Calcium and phosphorus** are important minerals of bone and any imbalance may result in developmental bone disease, signs of which may include bone enlargements at the knee and fetlock.

6 **Over-feeding** young growing horses for sales or training purposes is though to be a contributory factor in certain types of bone disease.

7 **Foals** may be given a creep feed with their dams, but this will depend on growth and development as well as grass availability and quality.

8 **Weaned foals** need balanced feeding with high protein levels (up to 18 per cent for growth) and this may be continued, depending on purpose and exercise.

9 **Calculate** energy requirements according to the type of work and amount of energy expended.

13 The Moving Horse

It is evident from all that has been said in this book that an organic horse is one produced to standards that will provide it with maximum growth, strength and health consistent with its genetic capability. Strong bone, as we keep repeating, is central to this. But it is also important to understand the dynamic nature of the horse, to appreciate what might lead to lameness, and therefore how to prevent it. This chapter discusses the principles that are fundamental to this objective.

▶ *Splints (the bony lumps visible) are a feature of the single digit*

▶ *The strain on the fetlocks and tendons is clearly demonstrated here*

Right at the beginning of this book we considered the evolutionary changes that turned the horse from the four-toed *Eohippus* to the single-toed animal of today; now we shall consider the influences of this, since inevitably the new construction has its disadvantages as well as its benefits. Amongst the immediate advantages were greater agility and speed, the change from four flattish toes to a rounded hoof bringing obvious improvements in lift-off and acceleration since the more upright conformation meant quicker pick-up from the toe, with the drive naturally coming from the powerful back end. Bigger horses with bigger bottoms meant more power, realised in either more speed or greater pulling strength, depending on muscle type. With the loss of three digits there were obviously fewer joints to injure, but the fact of the forces transferring to a single digit meant the development of a new set of priorities.

THE SINGLE DIGIT

The present digit represents, as we have already discussed, the middle finger of the human hand; it functions as a single entity and appears outwardly to be an uncomplicated anatomical unit – but the reality is different, because it is inherently weak. In fact the support given to the cannon by the vestigial second and fourth digits (the medial and lateral splint bones) is so important that surgical removal of the splints may lead to fracture of the cannon.

A 'splint' is a bony lump that develops between the splint bone and the cannon; it develops as a result of concussion or trauma, and is really an indication of the dependency of one structure on another. Splints are a frequent cause of lameness. More often than not, splints in adult animals result from an imbalance in the foot or limb, nothing more, and in most cases the problem is easily resolved by the farrier. The swelling and lameness simply demonstrate the importance of the relationship that exists between these structures.

The digit begins immediately below the knee (or carpus), which is in fact the equine equivalent of the human wrist; the title 'knee' is therefore incorrect by comparison to human anatomy, because in the horse, the equivalent of the human knee is the stifle.

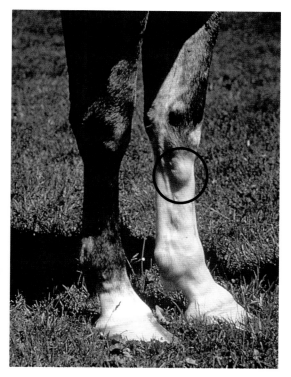

The Knee The horse's knee is a complex and strong structure, physically at its most vulnerable during the growing phases, before the horse reaches maturity. It consists of seven (sometimes eight) small bones set in two rows one above the other, and it makes up three joints including those between the radius above and the cannon below. In movement, the knee flexes as the forelimb is lifted from the ground, and it straightens as the toe is stretched forward for the next point of contact. The knee is subject to injury and lameness when poor conformation causes crunching between the small bones during strong movement (such as when landing from a jump). Fractures occur in horses that are 'back of the knee' – that is, of faulty conformation, such that were a line to be drawn vertically down through the centre of the limb when viewed from the side, the leg would describe a backward curve at the knee.

The Fetlock The single digit is really only single from the fetlock down, as there are no vestigial structures (like the splint bones) from here on. The fetlock is in itself a potentially weak point in the structure of the limb, firstly because of its angulation, and also because of the forces it has to support and absorb in movement. Unlike the knee which is supported from the structures above and below it, and by the ligaments that bind it, the fetlock is subjected to different stresses. Not only is there the effect of concussion when the foot strikes the ground – a stress borne in sequence by all the structures from the hoof upwards – but the fetlock is also particularly affected by the downward weight of the body, dropping significantly as weight comes over it, then recoiling to its natural position as the leg straightens up. Inevitably this effect is greatly exaggerated when the horse is landing from a jump, and it is at this point, typically, that any of the structures making up the joint might be injured.

The Tendons As the joint drops, the flexor tendons at the back of the lower front leg and the suspensory ligament (a vital support structure) are all stretched. While these are very resilient, injury to these structures is all too common – which just goes to show the weakness of the single digit when it is subjected to extreme forces in movement. Tendon injuries will also be sustained when the whole muscle/tendon unit loses elasticity; this can occur as a result of muscular injury, and clearly demonstrates the extent to which many limb structures are inter-related, and that injury to one often follows injury to another. This is a very important point when considering the cause of lameness.

The Sesamoids There are two sesamoid bones, situated at the back of the fetlock joint; they are bound there by a number of ligaments, including the suspensory ligament, and the flexor tendons are closely associated with their posterior surface. Sesamoid fractures are common, once again showing the high degree of stress that may be applied to the fetlock; also, because opposing forces tend to pull the damaged ends apart, sesamoids have always been considered difficult to treat.

Injuries to the pastern and the coffin (in the foot) joints result in damage to bone and ligaments, often causing permanent lameness. Fractures of the pastern are common in immature horses in training.

The Foot The horse's foot is a complex structure that was formerly thought to be the most common site of lameness. However, wider understanding would tend to refute this, although foot lameness is still very common and always needs to be considered when an animal is being examined. But it is important to be open-minded and to discount the idea that 90 per cent of lameness occurs in the foot, or at least beneath the knee, because there is a great deal that can go wrong above it.

Much foot lameness is the result of bad shoeing, and this also needs to be taken into account. Horse management affects the strength and texture of the horn, but a poorly balanced hoof can have repercussions further up the leg; faulty shoeing prac-

▼ *Natural hoof of a Dartmoor pony: in the wild, the unshod hoof takes on a short, rounded, tough shape; (right) hoof of a shod horse with hoof dressing. Correct farriery is vital; much foot lameness results from bad shoeing*

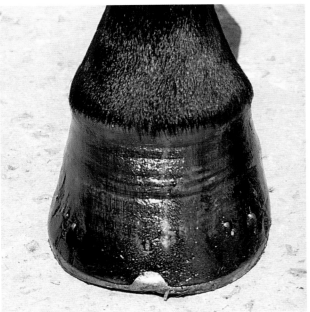

tice may also cause contraction of the foot because of lack of frog pressure; also bruising if the shoes come to bear on sensitive tissues.

In the wild, the unshod foot takes on a hardness that protects its inner structures from injury. It also takes on a shape that is short, rounded and tough; there is no abnormal spreading, and no spare horn because it is worn down in use. Its shape is designed to take weight on the bars and on the outer sides of the toes; it does its own trimming and keeps its own perfect balance. A modern innovation has been the introduction of four-point shoeing, intended to benefit the horse on the basis of this natural influence. This may not prove to be a good idea, however, because, as with stabling, we change the ground rules when we fit shoes and it may be that the whole wall is critical in weight bearing in the shod foot. There is a tendency for the new shoes to cause bruising at the toe, and balancing can also be a problem.

Laminitis is essentially a condition of domestication. Extremely painful, it may even be terminal, sometimes causing severe disruption of the attachments between the horn and the underlying bone. It occurs in conjunction with conditions such as retained afterbirth, and it can also result from severe concussion, from over-tight shoeing, and from grain engorgement and when grazing rich young grasses.

The navicular bone is another sesamoid bone situated at the back of the pedal bone. It is thought to be a source of concussive lameness in horses ridden on hard surfaces. However, there is a great deal of dispute relating to its significance, particularly since in many diagnosed cases, alternative sources of lameness exist, obscuring the part played by this condition in the overall scheme of things.

THE HIND LIMB

Lameness in the hind limb from the hock down is often similar in character to that suffered in the forelimbs, except with a lower incidence. The conditions seen are essentially the same; the lower incidence may well result from the fact that two-thirds of the bodyweight is carried by the front legs. The foot and pastern in the hind limb is more upright and is subject to less concussion as most weight is on the forelegs; but the hind limb contains the driving strength of the animal, and all forward impulsion is derived from behind. This power – especially when explosive movement such as jumping is involved – is generated through the musculature in the pelvic area as well as through the action of the hock and stifle, and the ligaments and bones on which all these structures work. This is reflected in the nature and incidence of lamenesses seen.

THE SPINE

The bony spine and its overlying muscles are likely to be heavily involved in lameness. The degree to which chiropractic, osteopathy and physiotherapy have expanded is proof of this, and the reason is explained by the anatomical construction of the horse. As is evident, the horse was never designed as a jumping animal: compared to the flea, or even the cat and dog, the height it can jump is unimpressive, but the effect on such a heavy animal of explosive effort of this sort is frequent disruption of the anatomical structures of the back.

▲ *This picture shows how much the neck can bend*

The greatest degree of movement in the spine occurs in the neck, where there is side-to-side and up-and-down movement as well as independent flexion, extension and rotation of the head. The horse can bring its muzzle round to its shoulder on either side with relative ease; it can scratch its ribs, flanks and quarters with its teeth, and this despite a fairly rigid trunk. The neck acts as a counterbalance while the horse is in movement, swinging and bobbing, especially when it is rebalancing itself after the effort of jumping; and of course it supports the head. The neck (and other) vertebrae contain the spinal cord, which is the direct communication between the brain and the body; it is also the centre of many reflexes that operate in relation to movement. Not surprisingly, locomotory problems that involve the neck can have far-reaching effects for the horse.

The thoracic vertebrae are basically rigid as a unit; while movement between vertebrae is limited, it is nonetheless sufficient to cause sources of pain, though this can be relieved by manipulation. There is greater, if still limited, movement between the individual lumbar vertebrae, although the real flexion of this part of the back occurs at the lumbo-sacral junction (which marks the beginning of the pelvis behind the saddle). It is the primary joint that bends as the horse arches its back, and therefore a common site of injury. Strains of muscles and ligaments occur, and they happen mostly as a result of exaggerated movements while the horse is being ridden or jumping – for instance when it slips, rears or falls.

The sacral vertebrae are fused and allow for little or no movement between segments (though fusion is incomplete in some adults); however the sacrum as a whole and its pelvic attachments are vulnerable to disruption. The sacrum forms a joint with the ilium called the sacro-iliac joint, and the very fact of this joint's existence indicates the capacity for a degree of movement between the sacrum and the rest of the pelvis.

The sacrum sits as the roof of the pelvic canal, attached by a number of ligaments, some in the form of wide sheets between the bony structures. In the mare, the pelvic ligaments have the capacity to soften, thus allowing the size of the canal to increase as the foal traverses it in the birth process; this is further indication that this is not a solid, immovable attachment. These ligaments also provide a site of origin for some of the major muscles of the upper quarter, meaning there is always a prospect of disruption to these, too, when an animal suffers a pelvic injury.

The manner of sacral attachment, except for the small sacro-iliac joint, is all by soft tissues, ligaments and muscle, and it is not uncommon for these to be injured, particularly in younger animals; over-difficult or excessively steep gallops are also causing injury with increasing frequency. Such damage is marked by a physical distortion of the external anatomy, by tissue pain, and by changes in action and movement. In most cases the problem is an expression of soft tissue injury and little else, although fractures do sometimes occur. Lameness resulting from damage to the sacro-iliac joint is unproven; there is reason to believe it is a minor factor, if indeed it is ever involved at all, the evidence being that horses which show injuries here respond fully to treatment in which the sacro-iliac joint is not moved, injected or otherwise interfered with. The symptoms seen in many such cases would have to include the possibility of sacro-iliac involvement, but it is appropriate to suggest that this does not occur in isolation and without disruption of other associated structures. This is, of course, anecdotal; as also is any evidence that the joint causes lameness.

Until any relationship between sacro-iliac joint disease and lameness is established objectively, the use of tissue-destroying drugs as a form of treatment should be discontinued. Not only is such treatment unlikely to have any benefit (if the person injecting it can actually reach the joint, which is in a very secluded position), but it can do untold harm and cause acute pain when placed in healthy tissues. From a pathological viewpoint, it makes very little sense that there would be abnormality in the sacro-iliac joint without movement of the sacrum relative to its attachments. It is also unlikely that pain from this joint would cause lameness rather than pain caused by soft tissue disruption. The idea that gross anatomical changes (and lameness) will be altered by obliterating these joints is in itself somewhat fanciful. Such treatments do not restore normal action where this has been lost, so they are unlikely to advance the animal's

▼ *The lumbo-sacral joint here is bent downwards at take-off, though the opposite will happen as the horse rounds over the jump*

chances of staying sound in the longer term. All they achieve is to provide a period of enforced rest when the underlying problems may settle and become less painful, though they will not regain full normality without more appropriate treatment.

Lameness of Spinal Origin It is not exaggerating to suggest that every jumping horse is likely to suffer spinal lameness at some time in its career. The source of pain relates directly to the bones of the spine and to the nerves that emerge from between them; pressure on these nerves is inevitably the cause of the pain, such that it interferes with conduction and usually results in an alteration to surface anatomy and movement. The problem generally arises because of movement between the spinal bones, but it is quite treatable by a trained chiropractor, for example. The damage is not usually accompanied by other soft tissue injuries, although it can be, in which case manipulation of the bones will need to be accompanied by soft tissue treatment.

Many horses suffer this sort of problem so regularly that a routine of preventive measures is built into their training programme: they are seriously inhibited in their ability to perform when feeling back pain, and are probably unable to jump or gallop without discomfort. Even non-jumping horses – those involved in dressage or Flat racing, for example – will experience a certain level of suffering when working if the spine is sore or painful.

The type of pain referred to is not completely crippling, as would be expected with spinal fractures, dislocations or other physical disruptions. These are all acute injuries that cause greater pain and are of a much more serious nature; they are detected clinically, and confirmed by methods such as radiography and scintigraphy. If treatable at all, they require specific consideration and complete rest. The lesser conditions are relieved by manipulation and the affected horse will be expected to be back in full work within days. The problem is comparable to human back pain: the source is the same, and the cause, and relief by manipulation is equally effective in both cases.

MUSCULAR INJURIES

Probably just as common, muscular injuries are very limiting. Years ago all horses were strapped during grooming: it was the accepted way of caring for the muscular system, and it acknowledged the importance of massage in keeping it supple and injury free. Sadly the demands of time have put an end to strapping – and at what cost?

Muscular injuries are as common now as they were in the past, but they are often ignored, either because they are not noticed, or because the associated lameness passes off in the course of a couple of days; besides, the pain is generally relieved by drugs such as phenylbutazone (bute). The horse returns to work – but many riders fail to notice that there is a change of action, albeit only slight – and this is where the real trouble lies: the damage might be no more than a minor tear in a single muscle, but the real problem is not simply that the injured muscle is not used properly, being painful, but that the action is changed. The same thing happens in human muscle injuries, except the horse cannot tell us of its problem: basically, when it returns to exercise, this (even small) change in action can lead to injury in other muscles that are obliged to take up the added strain, and cannot cope with it. It can also lead to sprains of joints and ligaments remote from the original injury, specifically because limb placement on the ground is in itself changed.

Treatment If the horse is to return to full normality, the original injury has to be treated, and the simplest way to do this is through conventional physiotherapy techniques. If the muscle is accessible and the injury close to the surface of the body, it is possible that strapping (or massage) might resolve it over a period of days. However, the idea that deep-seated injuries can be resolved by manual means does not hold up in practice. As a rule, modern equipment (mostly designed for human patients) used by physiotherapists does not wholly resolve the full extent of many of these lesions. While there is improvement and some measure of pain relief, the injuries are not actually repaired, and often tend to recur when the animal returns to work.

Strapping is a useful procedure for keeping the muscles supple and so less prone to injury

Human athletes who suffer similar injuries are impeded in their careers until they are treated and the damaged muscle returned to full working effectiveness. Horses suffer injuries particularly to the neck and shoulder muscles, also to the back and quarters; the muscles most affected in front are those lifting the shoulder and the elbow, but injuries in the pelvic region are more extensive and deep, usually involving those muscles deep in the heart of the upper surface of the quarter. Presumably these injuries also involve the deeper ligaments and their attachments (though this would be impossible to establish in a live animal). They respond to physiotherapy and controlled exercise over a period of weeks. They are seriously disadvantaged by swimming, which causes continued aggravation, and are not helped by cantering or galloping.

Injury usually affects one side only, though there is often pain on the opposite side, due to distortion caused by the uneven pull on bony structures and compensatory overuse of the sound side. There is also often injury to muscles on the diagonal forelimb, especially where the pelvic injury has existed for some time: this is a normal reaction to increased loading.

Muscular injuries have become increasingly common in all kinds of jumping horse; however, they are not always due to the sport *per se*, but are more often associated with the nature of the gallops used in training – the stiffness, the surface and the gradient, as well as the pace and the amount of work given per session. Damage often begins when the horse is unfit and training is in its early stages, though the influence may not be noticed until considerably later. While these may be significantly crippling conditions, some horses still manage to perform with them, though they are unsound for purchase. The influence is least dangerous on flat surfaces, or when competing against inferior horses at an easy pace for the affected animal; it is most dangerous in high-class competition when there is no room for error, and when the pace is pressing the horse's ability to perform to its limits.

The Picture in Detail Muscle is an elastic tissue that exerts its influence by its ability to stretch and contract; when injured, it loses this ability. It has a well organised nerve supply, and therefore plenty of pain receptors, which are triggered when tissue is torn. The consequence of pain is to avoid using the injured part, and without clinical help the torn tissues do not heal, and there is a tendency to fibrous repair. The muscle stays out of use and the injury compares to the kind of knot found in a human pulled muscle. The only difference is the size of the tear, its depth from the skin, and the consequences of not treating it. Whereas a human athlete with a pulled leg muscle has only one other leg to stand on, a horse has three – three more to injure, as it sometimes does.

Injury to neck muscles causes noticeable changes in the way the forelimbs are moved forwards. It might also cause a horse to hang or to jump to one side when ridden, or to resent passive movement to the affected side; it may also interfere with its ability to correct itself when it needs to. It can cause it to make jumping mistakes, and maybe to lose balance.

FITNESS AND PHYSICAL DEVELOPMENT DURING TRAINING

It is well recognised that racing two-year-olds places a huge risk of injury on their immature frame, and indeed many fail to stand up to the stresses involved. Bone fractures occur, as well as other types of lameness that may curtail a career. This is why conformation is critical when buying two-year-olds, as horses without enough bone are more likely to have problems, as will those that are too upright through their joints, meaning the effects of concussion are increased.

It is imperative that the process of training any horse is gradual and that all body systems are given time to adapt: in a progressive manner the heart must become more efficient at pumping blood, the circulation to vital tissues must be increased, and the lungs must develop the capacity for greater gas exchange. More red blood cells are needed to transport more oxygen; bone and ligaments must strengthen to withstand the increased stresses placed on them; and muscle – especially bulky upper body muscle

> ## FACTORS LIKELY TO INFLUENCE LAMENESS
>
> ■ Ground conditions, whether too hard, soft, holding or insecure.
> ■ Exceptionally steep inclines.
> ■ Sharp round gallops.
> ■ Adverse camber.
> ■ Jumping.
> ■ Excessive work and too fast a pace for unfit horses.
> ■ Ignored or undiagnosed muscular and spinal conditions.

– must strengthen to prepare itself for the task of propelling the body forwards at speed and perhaps over challenging obstacles.

Exercising Ground A major factor in limb injuries relates to ground conditions: the type of surface, how firm it is, how soft, the footing provided – all are important as causes of lameness. Inevitably, hard surfaces increase concussion and because of their unyielding nature, they can contribute to tendon injury; heavy ground may have the same effect because the horse becomes fatigued. Most critical, however, is the grip a surface provides, as any movement in a surface causes instability when the limb is taking weight. Many horses express their lack of confidence in a loose surface by not committing themselves – they won't work freely and may refuse to jump – but those that do, often suffer injury to joints or to the muscles, ligaments and bones in the upper body structures.

The gradient of a gallop is also an important element in causing lameness. While it has always been correctly assumed that working horses on an upward gradient takes weight from the forelimbs and reduces concussion, the effort when it is too steep can affect other areas. Notably there is an increase in quarter muscle injuries as well as pelvic fractures.

Round gallops can lead to lameness if they are not intelligently used; if only ridden in one direction, muscle tends to develop more on one side than the other, and injuries ensue. Also, if used at pace, joint injuries are common.

VETERINARY MEDICINE AND THE LAME HORSE

Technological changes within this field have brought a whole new approach to lameness diagnosis. Tendon injuries are assessed by ultrasound scanning, bone injuries through methods such as scintigraphy (substances are injected that concentrate in damaged bone, which is then located by a special camera), and efforts are being made to diagnose spinal conditions based on thermography. A variety of methods are being used to analyse gait in an effort to identify changes in normal movement, and thereby locate the source of lameness. All of these advances reflect a sea-change in both teaching and clinical medicine.

At the time of writing there are only about 250 full-time horse vets in Britain, so it is clearly a small field. Clinicians do not, on the whole, write papers, or have time for research, or teach, with the result that time-honoured skills are being lost; moreover the academic world cannot teach what it does not inherently possess. Hence the need for technology – but technology is of no use except in the hands of experienced and mature operatives; otherwise the equipment, or some remote laboratory, is being asked to make a diagnosis which the practising vet can neither support nor refute.

An extreme consequence of this is the use of local analgesia (nerve blocks) in the diagnosis of lameness. They are geared to the idea that most lameness occurs below the knee, a professional way of shooting in the dark, as the process of eliminating particular areas is not based on perception, heat changes or swelling, as was always the case in the past. Now these signs are ignored if the nerve block does not affect them, and medicine becomes increasingly confused. The practice leaves itself open to legal challenge when the cause of lameness exists above the area blocked (which is quite often); a competent professional should be obliged to know, and this path to diagnosis is not acceptable unless there is strong reason to believe that lameness comes from the area being anaesthetised.

Following the organic ideal should enable our horses to have a more enjoyable lifestyle

The extent to which technology is abused is highlighted by research which suggests that since almost all horses have asymmetrical limbs, they should have special shoes to make them all the same length. This proposal must be disputed on the grounds that without knowing what clinical factors might create such a discrepancy, it is hardly objective.

WHAT YOU CAN DO

UNDERSTANDING THE MOVING HORSE

1 **Be aware** of the inherent weaknesses of the single digit and apply this knowledge in order to prevent lameness and avoid injury.

2 **Foot and limb balance** are critical to soundness and it is important that any manner of shoeing does not disturb overall limb balance.

3 **Be careful** with four-point shoeing that the result is not sole pressure leading to lameness.

4 **The sesamoid bones** and their ligamentous attachments are frequently involved in fetlock injuries; diagnosis is with X-rays and treatment best served by appropriate physiotherapy coupled with support and rest.

5 **Tendon injuries** are commonly a result of horses being galloped with existing muscular injuries; any sensible form of treatment should take this into account.

6 **Care of the muscles** was reflected in the widespread practice of strapping in the past; there is a need to return to that type of thinking.

7 **The back and muscular system** are vital in modern lameness and it is probable that the influence of interval training coupled with stiffer gallops has led to a higher incidence of injury to both.

8 **Our understanding of lameness** arising from the spine and pelvis has resulted in the expansion of manipulative services which are essential both in diagnosis and treatment.

9 **Pelvic fractures** are more common on steep gallops; most recover with proper care and rest.

10 **Racing** has a rising proportion of horses with pelvic or hind-leg lamenesses; these conditions are diagnosable and treatable and there is a need for some action to be taken to prevent the abuse of these animals.

Bibliography

Botham, P.A. 'Are pesticides immunotoxic?' (*Adverse Drug Reactions & Acute Poisoning Reviews*, Vol 9[2] [pp91–101], 1990)

Budiansky, Stephen 'Too fast to get faster' (*US News & World Report*, 28 April 1997)

Caldwell, Gladys 'Fluoride, the Smoking Gun in Acid Rain' (*The American Sunbeam*, November 1982)

Cartwright, Frederick F. *Disease in History* (Mentor, 1971)

Clutton-Brock, Juliet *Domesticated Animals from Early Times (8, Horses)* (Heinemann/British Museum/Natural History)

Code of Good Agricultural Practice for the Protection of Water (MAFF, 1991)

DeCrosta, Anthony 'Learn to Live without Chlorine' (*Organic Gardening*, December 1978)

Elliott, Mark BVSc, VetMFHom, MRCVS 'Nutraceutical Medicine' (*Veterinary Times*, July 1998)

Elsworth, Steve *Acid Rain* (Pluto Press, 1984)

Eustace, Robert A. BVSc, MRCVS *Explaining Laminitis and its Prevention* (1992)

Fitzwygram *Horses and Stables* (Longmans, Green and Co, 1894)

Flint, Carl (ed) *Crops – Guide to Herbicides* (Reed Business Publishing, 1987)

Frame, John *Improved Grassland Management* (Farming Press Books, 1992)

Frape, David *Equine Nutrition and Feeding* (Longman Scientific and Technical, 1986)

Georgi and Georgi *Parasitology for Veterinarians* (Saunders, 1990)

Gordon, Stuart *Down the Drain* (MacDonald Optima, 1989)

Grant, Doris 'Fluoride: The Poison in Our Midst' (*The Ecologist* Vol 16, No 6, 1986)

Gray, Peter *Diseases of the Digestive System* (J.A. Allen & Co Ltd, 1998)

—— *Lameness* (J.A. Allen & Co Ltd, 1994)

—— *Parasites and Skin Diseases* (J.A. Allen & Co Ltd, 1995)

—— *Respiratory Disease* (J.A. Allen & Co Ltd, 1994)

Hanway, J.J., J.B. Herrick, T.L. Willrich, P.C. Bennett & J.T. McCall *The Nitrate Problem* (Special Report No 34, Iowa State University of Science and Technology, 1963)

Herd, Rupert P. MVSc, PhD Parasite control in horses: 'Pasture sweeping' (*Modern Veterinary Practice*, 1986 67 [12] [pp893-894])

—— 'Pasture hygiene: a non-chemical approach to equine endoparasite control' (*Modern Veterinary Practice*, 1986 67[1] [pp36-38])

Horserace Betting Levy Board Common Codes of Practice (1995)

Jeffcott, L.B. 'Osteochondrosis in the horse – searching for the key to pathogenesis' (*Equine Veterinary Journal* [1991] 23 [5] 331–338)

Lampkin, Nicolas *Organic Farming* (Farming Press Books, 1990)

Lean, Geoffrey & Don Hinrichsen *WWF Atlas of the Environment* (Helicon Publishing Ltd, 1990/1992)

Lees, Andrew and McVeigh, Karen *An Investigation of Pesticide Pollution in Drinking Water in England and Wales* (Friends of the Earth Water Pollution and Toxics Campaign, 1988)

Mayhew's Illustrated Horse Management, revised by J.I. Lupton MRCVS (Wm H. Allen & Co, 1876)

Miles, W.J. MRCVSL *Modern Practical Farriery* (William MacKenzie, undated)

Nutrient Requirements of Horses (National Academy Press, 1989)

Palmeria, C.M., A.J. Moreno, V. Bairos & V.M.C. Madeira 'Structural alterations in isolated hepatocytes induced by the herbicides paraquat, dinoseb and 2,4-D' (*Medical Science Research* Vol 25[5] [pp339–342], 1997)

Pearce, Fred *Acid Rain* (Penguin, 1987)

Pedersen, B.K. & H. Bruunsgaard 'How physical exercise influences the establishment of infections' (*Sports Medicine* Vol 19[6] [pp 393–400], 1995)

Pope, Stephen, Mike Appleton & Elizabeth-Anne Wheal *The Green Book* (Hodder and Stoughton, 1991)

Peters, E.M. 'Exercise, immunology and upper respiratory tract infections' (*International Journal of Sports Medicine*, Supplement, Vol 18[1] [pp 69–77], 1997)

Prescott, Ann 'What's the Harm in Aluminium' (*New Scientist*, 21 January 1989)

Rossdale, Peter *The Horse from Conception to Maturity* (J.A. Allen & Co Ltd, 1993)

Sanford, Paul A. *Digestive System Physiology* (Edward Arnold, 1982)

The Soil Association Symbol Scheme – Standards for Organic Food and Farming (1993)

Thomas, Dr J.A. 'Drugs and chemicals that affect the endocrine system' (*International Journal of Toxicology* Vol 17[2] [pp129–138], 1998)

Walters, A.H. *Clinical Ecology in Environmental Health* Vol V, No 3 (1985)

Water Pollution from Farm Waste (1987 England and Wales), (Water Authority Association, April 1989)

Zahradnik, Fred *Nitrates: A Needless Danger* (US 1983)

Index